EMPOWERED
LIFE™

EMPOWERED LIFE™

The 10 Core Palumbo Principles

NATASHA M PALUMBO

Eternal Enterprise Publishing

Empowered Life

First Printing: 2020

ISBN-13: 978-1-7344905-3-4

Cover Design: Joanne Jenkins and Natasha Palumbo with Ldy Bug Images
Author Bio Photograph: Juan Padilla with Luxus Photos
Editing & Interior Design: Lauren Michelle

Eternal Enterprise Publishing
Sacramento, CA Ordering Information:

Special discounts are available on quantity purchases by corporations, associations, educators, and others. For details, contact the publisher at the above listed address.

U.S. trade bookstores and wholesalers:
Please contact Natasha M Palumbo:
www.natashapalumbo.com

To my beautiful children, Allan and Annabella.
I love you both forever and always.

Acknowledgments

Father God, I thank You for the beautiful gift of life, Your eternal love, and amazing grace. Without You, I am nothing. But through You, I am Natasha M Palumbo, the daughter of the Most High. All honor and glory to Your name.

To my best friend, Joanne Jenkins, thank you for being the one true person outside of my children that I trust with all of me. Thank you for all the support, not only for the time you have given to me during the writing of my book, but for all the constant support in my life. I am grateful for you. You are not only my best friend, you are my sister.

To my earthly angel, who will remain unnamed, you completely saved me and blessed me abundantly. I am eternally grateful, and I pray you receive a thousand-fold back for all you have done for me. Thank you is simply not enough, but for now it will have to do.

Note to the Reader

Dear reader, I want to thank you for your support. The fact that you are reading this book tells me that you are ready to live the *Empowered Life*. I pray the wisdom you find inside these pages will help guide you in your life so that you may be EMPOWERED and live in your full authentic self.

I am in the business of building up people. This book is a tool to help build you up. I host workshops and events that, if you attend, you will leave a different person than when you came. To learn more about me and the services I offer, you may visit my website at the address listed below. I am a business adjunct professor for several colleges in the state of California, as well as a coach and consultant. I have been an entrepreneur since 2002. I have now authored a total of three books and one workbook. *Entrepreneurship Empowered* is a business guide, one that tells my story of going from being a welfare mom to the CEO of a thriving company. There is a companion workbook that goes along with the book and helps bring your business to life. *IMPACT!* is the second book in my Empowerment series, and it is the story of my philanthropic work as it relates to social entrepreneurship.

I am open and public with my story, and you will now be able to learn more about me and how I took my trauma and turned it into triumph. I live the Empowered Life and the life of an influencer. The gift I give is the gift of self. Once you have *you* back, everything will fall into place. I would love for you to connect with me. You may find me on both LinkedIn and Instagram @ Natasha M Palumbo.

Be well,
Natasha M Palumbo, MBA

Author, Coach, Consultant, and Speaker
Entrepreneur – Educator – Empowered
www.natashapalumbo.com

Contents

INTRODUCTION

"I love those who can smile in trouble, who can gather strength from distress, and grow brave by reflection. 'Tis the business of little minds to shrink, but they whose heart is firm, and whose conscience approves their conduct, will pursue their principles unto death."

—Leonardo da Vinci, Renaissance genius

As an artist myself, I admire the work of Leonardo da Vinci. Not to mention he is Italian, like me. The quote above is right on the money. The 10 Core Palumbo Principles I personally pursue unto death, and now I am going to share them with you. My belief, however, transcends death and moves into eternal life. I am currently building my final empire, which is the Eternal Enterprise, and by doing so, I capture eternal life. No longer will these principles be pursued only unto death. They will be shared with the world, and they will guide my seeds into seeds forevermore. This, my friends, is how you not only break generational curses, this is how you plant generational blessings. This is what I call the *Empowered Life.*

I come from a deep history of poverty, abuse, and neglect. The first two decades of my life, most humans would have never made it out of. But today, I share my message of hope and inspiration with all who will listen and receive me. I can be a hard pill to swallow, but I can also help you transform. I will awaken you if you are ready. If you are not, I plant good seed and I believe in it. I am matrix-free, and although I visit the matrix often, I am not one of them. I look like an agent, but I am really a glitch and I know the escape route. I am on a mission to serve and love others deeply and to share the truth about trauma and its effects on the body, the bloodline, and the soul. I live an Empowered Life, but it took a lot of work to get here. It was not easy, but it was worth it. I wish I could say that I have done all the work I need to be free of my trauma, but that is not the case. Trauma comes with side effects, some of the worst ever. And trauma breeds trauma. Trauma also attracts trauma. So, I continued to suffer long after the first two decades of my life. I am now forty-five years of age, and it has only been in the last five years or so that I have truly come to love myself. And the last three years have been the most powerful in my healing and transformation.

I used to weigh over 300 hundred pounds. You see, of-tentimes, we carry our trauma physically. Did you know that ninety percent of our health issues come from trau-ma? Truth be told, I'm surprised I'm as healthy as I am today. This is the power of my mind and my determina-tion to not die with the demons—to break the curses and plant the blessings. After seven years of in-depth EMDR therapy, I was finally able to peel back the layers of my trauma and fully begin to love myself. This newfound self-love manifested in many forms: one of which was my weight loss. I lost over a hundred pounds. I went from a size 24 to a size 8. Say what?! Self-love in action. I finally did right by food.

There is an equation I am going to share with you now regarding weight loss. Are you ready? Eighty percent mental, nineteen percent food, and one percent workout. You are going to see that mindset is everything when it comes to living the Empowered Life. You must get your mind right or *you* will never be right. You cannot work out a bad diet. You must eat right and clean. You must also be consistent. The body thrives off of consistency. Yes, it can be boring to eat the same healthy thing every day, but it is the best way to live if you are striving for weight loss and good health.

Because I had done the deep work of trauma therapy, I was truly ready to let go of the old me and receive the new me. I am yet again on the path of receiving another new me. I want you to stop trying to get the old you back.

You don't want the old you. You always want the new you. Don't go backward, only forward. Many times, we are so busy holding on to things of the past that we are not able to receive what is awaiting us in the present and future. I am learning this principle now as I am yet again working on losing more weight. You see, I kept the weight off for a long time, but then I stopped doing right by the food. It took a bit of time, but then, boom! I had gained some weight back. Now mind you, I have not gained very much back, but it was enough for me to become disappointed with myself.

I worked so hard and finally got that new body and was like, *"Hallelujah, who are you?"* Then I became comfortable and started slacking off when it came to food. I slowly gained a little weight back, and then something else happened that I didn't see coming: I went back to body shaming. Men and women can be very hard on themselves regarding their appearance. Damn society. Do we keep blaming society, though? Or do we stand flat-footed and look in the mirror and say enough is enough? You are wonderfully and beautifully made. Now get it together. If you don't like something about yourself, then change it.

I realized that I must be hurting again. Why was this voice in my head saying these hurtful words? Why was I not seeing myself in the light I know myself to be? I had been out of therapy for a bit of time. I mean, come on, after seven years of in-depth trauma therapy, you'd think

I'd be good to go. Well, I wasn't. So back to therapy I went. I said to myself, *"Listen here, you are going to need to toughen up, buttercup, and go back and get more help. There is absolutely nothing wrong with getting more help. For goodness sake, you are the cheerleader of getting the help you need. I am going to need you to 'ra ra' for yourself right about now."* And that is what I did. I want you to understand something, my dear one. You must be your greatest cheerleader and your toughest coach because NO ONE IS COMING TO SAVE YOU! Yes, I just yelled that at you. Because I need you to fully grasp that, especially because you are going to live an Empowered Life, and it is up to you to do so.

I am now seeing another wonderful therapist. I am in a different type of trauma therapy, one that involves art and brainspotting, a sister therapy to EMDR. When I found my new therapist, I knew it was a perfect fit. As I stated in the first sentence of this book, I am an artist. Art is extremely healing, and I have used it for a long time. I encourage you to use art to help you heal, too. I also want to express to you the importance of mental health. There is nothing wrong with getting the help you need. You will stop throwing up on people. You will transform. You will heal. And, more importantly, you will live in freedom. Mind you, freedom comes in pieces. Depending on how much trauma you have endured and how determined you are to do the work, you may need to be in therapy for a while. I have realized that after many years of work, and I still need to do more. This is one of the hardest pills to swallow—but swallow it, I will. I have tasted freedom. True freedom. I cannot, nor will I ever, turn back. I am not going to die with these demons. I am not going to suffer my entire life. I am going to do the work that is needed to live my life and to live it EMPOWERED!

I want to be clear with you that healing yourself takes a lot of work. It is going to be ugly. It is going to hurt. You will work your ass off and still need to do more. This will suck. But then you will begin to feel lighter. You will let go of people, places, and things that are toxic to you, and life will not hurt as much. You may miss these people, places, and things, but you will realize you don't need them. Your vibration will rise, and you will become intoxicated by the joy that is found at a vibration you never even knew existed. You are going to set boundaries to protect yourself. If those boundaries offend others, that is on them, not you. They are your boundaries, and you have rights to them. If you struggle with setting boundaries, I am hopeful that by the time you finish this book, you will not only have them set, you will be fully operating out of them.

I have endured much in my life. I will share more and more of me as I move you through the 10 Core Palumbo Principles. My hope is that you will not only receive inspiration from these principles and the stories found within, but you will be encouraged to write your own truth and share your story with the world—especially if you have endured great trauma and hardships. We need your story. There is a sea of people you are called to, and they need you to heal yourself and then move forward in your position of power. Please know your suffering is not in vain. I promise! I used to ask God all the time: "Why so much? Why do I have to endure so many things? Dear Lord, when is enough, enough?"

He responded, "I am making you more relatable."

"Don't you think I am relatable enough?"

"No, my beloved. But you are almost there."

You see, suffering is necessary until it is no longer necessary. Because I suffered, I get to see things most people will never ever get to see. Because I suffered, I get to live a ridiculously amazing life, one that most people will never live. Because I suffered, I get to serve and love others deeply and with a fire that burns within me, one that I truly believe will live forevermore. I get to help set the captives free. That is my gift—the greatest one I have to give outside of love. I have an extraordinary God-given talent, which is to give others the gift of self. Yes, you read that right. I give you the keys to help you find yourself. And in doing so, I have given you everything you need. Like a domino effect, after you truly grasp hold of the gift of you, everything else will fall into place and you will live an Empowered Life.

In just a few moments, I am going to break down what you will find within this book. I have several call-to-action activities that will help you with personal growth and development. Anything you can do to grow within will continue to EMPOWER you. Empowerment means to take the keys to your life back—take the keys to your rights back. I want you to always be pursuing personal and professional development because we never arrive. We do grow and get stronger, absolutely, but I am a firm believer we can always strive to be better—to improve, to master our masteries.

Because of my tragic backstory, my life's work is trauma. I am truly honored to have this calling. I was chosen, and so were you. Each person walking this earth has a calling on their life. It is up to each one of us to walk in our calling, no matter how difficult it may be. I want you to not only walk in the calling of your life, I want you to live an Empowered Life. In order to do so, you need to understand the power of knowledge and research. We live in a world where people are not thinking for themselves. Listen, if you don't think for yourself, someone else will think for you.

I am going to ask that you take a deep dive into your mind—a deep dive into your soul. I have shared three different types of trauma therapies that I believe in. I am now going to explain a little more about each of them, so you have a better understanding. I will write about them throughout this book as I tell my story. They play a huge role in my success and ability to overcome. I cannot give you the gift of self without first giving you the tools you need to heal.

"Courage doesn't happen when you have all the answers. It happens when you are ready to face the questions you have been avoiding your whole life."

—Shannon L. Alder, inspirational author

The EMDR Institute defines EMDR as *"Eye Movement Desensitization and Reprocessing (EMDR). It is a psychotherapy treatment that was originally designed to alleviate the distress associated with traumatic memories."* I personally swear by EMDR. I know its power because I have experienced it. The mind may repress trauma or tuck it in a corner, but the body holds on to it. This is why trauma screening in the medical industry is so important. Doctor Nadine Burke Harris is a pediatrician in California and was appointed by Governor Gavin Newsom as the first California General Surgeon. According to an article written by Robert Waters with the California Health Care Foundation, *"In 2012, Dr. Burke Harris founded the Center for Youth Wellness, a national organization that raises awareness about the lifelong impact of adverse childhood experiences (ACEs) and trauma on the health and mental health of children. The concept of ACEs first* emerged from a 1998 study that found that children exposed to abuse, neglect, and other negative experiences had an increased lifelong risk of many common chronic health conditions. Burke Harris has pioneered the development of screening tools to assess children's exposure to ACEs and to treat them. Her TED talk on the effect of trauma on children has been viewed more than 5 million times."[1] If you haven't seen her TED Talk yet, I want you to find it and watch it. She is part of the reason why I plan to earn my doctoral degree by studying intergenerational trauma. There truly is a bloodline of trauma, and poverty is passed on. If this runs in your family, I want you to know it ends with you. You are going to break the curse and plant the blessing.

According to Psychology Today, "Art therapy involves the use of creative techniques such as drawing, painting, collage, coloring, or sculpting to help people express themselves artistically and examine the psychological and emotional undertones in their art. With the guidance of a credentialed art therapist, clients can 'decode' the nonverbal messages, symbols, and metaphors often found in these art forms, which should lead to a better understanding of their feelings and behavior so they can move on to resolve deeper issues."[2] I absolutely love art therapy. The walls in my house are covered with artwork—either in artistic photographs that I have taken or actual paintings that I've created. I have a K-12 education background. I was going to school to be a high school photography teacher. In order to do so, you need to be an art teacher. The color psychology of art is fascinating. I have a painting from my late twenties. It is a self-portrait. I remember my art teacher being taken aback by it as she examined the painting. She gasped as she looked at it and took a deep breath. "Interesting color choice, Natasha," she said. She then proceeded to give me some pointers on shading and the like.

As I grew in my knowledge of color psychology, I realized why she gasped the way she did. You could clearly see the pain in my portrait. I was hurting. Deeply. Today, I have the most beautiful self-portrait of what I call "*The Blue Lady.*" I just painted her this year. She is much lighter, full of happiness, loved, and she is the billionairess. She is me, and I am her. I strongly encourage you to pick up a brush. You might just find you a blue lady too. What I do know you'll find is freedom—if you allow yourself to let go and flow.

Brainspotting is a therapy I started this year. I am still processing this therapy. It is very intense. I am fascinated by the brain and all that we can do with it. Brainspotting deals with the stored experiences that are found in our minds and in our bodies. Again, you think you can just tuck the memory away, then someone walks by you and they smell a certain way and you just want to throw up. Or certain colors just happen to trigger you and set you off. These are just two examples of how trauma is stored in the body. According to an article written in

Depression Alliance, an online mental health resource, *"Brainspotting is a new model of psychotherapy created to help people overcome negative and traumatic emotions, physical trauma, as well as psychologically-induced physical pain. Brainspotting was created by David Grand, PhD, in 2003 as a result of his work with people who had experienced traumatic events such as Hurricane Katrina, the attacks on the World Trade Center, as well as war veterans. Many mental health professionals have found brainspotting to be an effective form of treatment for several mental health problems and physical illnesses. Brainspotting theory suggests that the brain can heal itself from inside. It aims to stimulate the brain's healing ability by evoking and releasing the negative emotions and experiences that have been stored in it. It does this by identifying an eye position that triggers and releases these emotions. This procedure is based on a concept that an individual's direction of gaze can affect how they feel. It lends to the theory that the eyes have an intense relationship with the brain. Furthermore, brainspotting is based on the fact that trauma is stored in the body and can be activated or triggered at a certain eye position."*[3]

I can attest to the power of this therapy. What surprised me about it was how much I experienced when going through a treatment. I was able to experience the past, present, and future. A door opened, and then another one, then another one. It was very intense, and I cannot do it each time I go. I am working through it at a slow pace. I use a combination of art therapy, brainspotting, and talk therapy on my current journey. Talk therapy is cool, but it doesn't move or release what is stored in the body or brain. Again, I have decades of trauma, and I also have a bloodline of it, too. So my work is not your work. But I hope that my work inspires you to do the work you need to do. It is only through therapy that I have been able to heal.

Before I move on to sharing the 10 Core Palumbo Principles, I would like to thank you for reading this book. My prayer is that you not only receive a wealth of information that helps you become EMPOWERED, but that it helps give way to your voice—your story. It took me many years to finally pull the muzzle off my mouth and live out loud. As you read the words of this book, I encourage you to take time and deeply digest, ponder, reflect, and give way to the future.

Chapter One is about your money. Because I come from a deep history of poverty, I have lived off bare bones for too damn long. But if you recall me telling you about *"The Blue Lady,"* well, she is a billionairess. She is me. I am open to receive. Money is energy. We live in an abundant world, but we must see it that way. If you see lack, then all you will have is lack. You must change your mindset to reap all of the riches that life has to offer. Poverty is passed on. If it was passed on to you, I want you to know you don't have to accept it, and you damn sure better not pass it on to your children.

Chapter Two is all about exploring the truth of emotions, specifically the power they have over us and our society. You will also learn how to exchange wounded emotion for emotional intelligence—or, as I like to call it, exchanging beauty for ashes. Emotional intelligence is central to living the Empowered Life. This chapter will be full just like the others, but I would ask you to really take time to do additional research when it comes to emotional intelligence. Learn all you can. Study those whose professions deal with teaching you how to be more emotionally intelligent. Intellect is wonderful, indeed, but emotional intelligence is far more powerful.

Chapter Three is all about grit. I am one gritty lady but had no clue what it meant until my mentor called me gritty one day. Grit is passion and perseverance—working toward our goals over a long period of time. To live the Empowered Life, you must be gritty. I think you will have a lot of fun with the call-to-action activities in this chapter.

Chapter Four is near and dear to my heart because I am a LION and all about results. We can plan and set goals all we'd like, but if we don't get to work, we have nothing. You are going to need to work in this life. And a willing worker will always have something to do. Execution is everything. I will give you some great strategies in this chapter that have personally helped me with execution. This book and the other three that I have written are just a few examples of how much I execute.

By the time this is published, I will have written and launched four books in slightly over one year—execution at its finest.

Chapter Five will require you to put your creative hat on. The reason being is that as EMPOWERED individuals, we don't predict our future; we create it. I am big on manifestation. I have vision boards everywhere— on my walls in my home to lock screens on my phone. I will, at the drop of a hat, create a vision board. Over my years of doing vision board work, I have seen many of the things on my boards appear. I have also learned how to tap in even deeper and make my board stronger. I not only bring in my thought, I also bring in my heart. I am going to need you to do the same when you create yours.

Chapter Six is going to give you some cold, hard truths. You are going to learn the power of sacrifice. It is mission-critical to breaking free and living in your authentic self. In order to truly live a ridiculously amazing life, you are going to need to sacrifice. I can promise you it will be worth it.

Chapters Seven and Eight are based on two books I have read and absolutely love. They are by Don Miguel Ruiz. He is a renowned spiritual teacher and a bestselling author. I have several of his books, and I recommend them to my students, clients, and the like. I am going to explain to you how I use them in my life and how they have helped me on my EMPOWERMENT journey.

Chapters Nine and Ten will close us out, and it is all me. I will be pouring out to you all I can before I leave you. Keep in mind that I am giving you the gift of self. The final chapters are going to be intense. You may even cry because I am going to have you do some soul-searching call-to-action activities in order to fully activate you before you go on your way. I end with the most powerful principles of them all, because, my dear ones, it is not how you start this life, but rather how you end it. I am expecting that you will all end EMPOWERED.

Welcome to *Empowered Life*.

O N E

PALUMBO PRINCIPLE 10:
PAY YOURSELF FIRST!

*"You must gain control over your money or the lack of it will
forever control you."*

—Dave Ramsey, author and financial guru

If you are going to live the Empowered Life, I need
you to understand that you must pay yourself first.
Clients and students come to me when they're
working on the financial part of their business, and, far
too often, they fail to add their salaries. Whether you
have the money to pay yourself or not, it doesn't matter.
You still need to allocate the money, and then when you
do have the actual funds on hand, you compensate
yourself. Paying yourself first, however, doesn't start in

business, but rather in your personal life. You should always take your paycheck and put a percentage of the money away for yourself—a savings if you will. It doesn't have to be a lot, just make sure you take something and put it away. *"But Professor, my lights are due and so is the rent. I only have enough to pay that."* I understand, but guess what? You must be disciplined and still put some money away for yourself. You need to have a "come-to-Jesus" moment and take a cold, hard look at your money, and even more so, your spending habits. You don't have a salary problem; you have a spending problem. When you pay yourself first, you are teaching yourself that saving is a priority and important to your future. You must know that you are worth paying yourself first.

Poverty is passed down. That, along with trauma, is one of the biggest generational curses around. However, I am a living witness that generational curses can be broken, and generational blessings can be planted. We must take possession of our birthright to abundance. We do not have to lack. Lack is an illusion. We live in a very abundant world, but there are controlling forces out there trying to keep us enslaved. The curse of poverty is a long-standing, controlling force. Look how long it has had your family line imprisoned. It is not going to be easy to break. It will, however, be worth it. I want you to understand that you have been chosen in this life to course-correct your ancestral line. *The way out is within.* You must go deep within and do the work that is required for you to not only be healed, but to be free. You will see me address *the way out is within* several times in this book. It is the most important Palumbo Principle, and its theme resides in all of my principles.

The mind is a powerful tool. Thoughts create our reality more than you could even begin to imagine. We are energy, and so are our thoughts. They reside on different vibrational energy levels. As a man thinks, so he shall be. There is no greater truth than this. The way you see money and the mindset you have regarding money is going to need to be examined.

Over the summer of 2019, I was able to attend a women's empowerment event in San Diego, California. One exercise we did was a guided meditation focused on money. We were asked to allow money to show itself to us, then report on it after the meditation. When the spirit of money first appeared to me, it appeared as bare bones. It was quite odd, to say the least. Then, that body of bones quickly began to morph into the most beautiful flowing light source. Have you ever seen a butterfly costume? The ones where the sleeves are wings? When you lift your hands, the wings appear. Well, this beautiful beaming body of light had just that. As it morphed into a body of light, it lifted its hands, and wings of light appeared. It flowed with incredible energy. It told me it was bigger than bare bones and it wanted to give me more. I pondered the exercise, and I realized that due to my family history of poverty, which became my story, too, I had learned to live off bare bones. My mind was still seeing bare bones, but before me was really an ever-flowing light source of money that wanted to give me more. Abundance had appeared, and a shift took place inside my mind. Another piece had arrived.

I want you to spend some time thinking about money and your relationship with it. How has your family history of money translated into your story? I encourage you to go into a meditated state to start the process and ask the spirit of money to appear to you. No pressure in how it appears, just allow what comes to come. You will find a set of questions to guide you along the way and space to write.

How did the spirit of money appear to you in your meditation, and did it have a message for you?

_____

_____

_____

_____

_____

_____

_____

_____

_____

What did you see in your family regarding money matters?

_____

_____

_____

_____

_____

_____

_____

_____

_____

_____

What are your current beliefs regarding money?

_____

_____

_____

_____

_____

_____

_____

_____

What would you like to see for your future regarding money?

_____

_____

_____

_____

_____

_____

_____

_____

_____

Acquiring money is not really all that hard. Keeping it and doing right by it, however, is. I was a welfare mom who was blessed with a business that took me from welfare to wealth overnight—literally. I went to bed on July 15, 2002 poor, and I woke up on July 16, 2002 the owner a thriving six-figure business. I grew that business into five states and thirty locations. I was not playing. I was ready for my wealth—or so I thought. But I still had a survival mindset. The survival mindset will have you forever stuck in poverty. Meaning, I lived in a house with no furniture, yet I had thousands upon thousands of dollars in the bank. I didn't know how to handle all that money. I didn't pay myself. I just picked at the money. I took what I needed when I needed it. I was giving to others and not myself. I have one of the biggest hearts around. Giving gifts to others is part of my love language.

I can remember Dan, the man I bought my business from, coming to see me around Christmas the first year I owned my business. I had the biggest tree ever, and there were presents that covered my entire living room floor. I can still hear him now: "Wow, Natasha, that is a beautiful tree. And so many gifts. But where is your furniture?" My response: "I am finally able to give quality gifts to those I love." He said, "But what about you?"

It took me almost fifteen years from that point to finally think about me. Don't lose that much time. How old are you? Now how long have you been subjecting yourself to the weight of others? Gifting to everyone else but not to yourself? I know I did it for far too long. I did it because I sought love. I thought, *If I give to you, you will love me.* BULLSHIT!

I'm so glad I woke up. Now I am in pursuit to help others wake up too. Mindset matters. You can rewire your mind. It has taken me years to rewire mine—and I am still a work in progress—but I am certainly much further than where I was. Today, I operate out of an abundant mindset. With this mindset, I know I have no lack. I know that I don't have to give away who I am to others in hopes that they will love me. I understand the importance of gratitude and its relationship to having more.

"When you are grateful, fear disappears and abundance appears."

—Tony Robbins, author and life coach

I am constantly giving thanks for my abundance. Each month, I write an abundance letter and give thanks for all I desire. I want you to know that abundance is not just money. Oh no, it is so much more. I give thanks for all kinds of abundance—from nail growth to love to trips to creativity, the list goes on and on. The key to my success with activating abundance is I don't worry about when it will come. Instead, I remain fully confident that I have everything I need when I need it. With this new mindset, I have found that I live a fuller life. I want you to do all you can to research and learn how to live in an abundant mindset. The damn survival mindset will have you doing all kinds of things you don't want to do. It feeds your trauma. It will keep you bound to the curse. But the abundant mindset will open the door to your freedom, and from it, you will be able to learn how to create greater wealth—generational wealth.

I am now going to give you one last call-to-action activity for this chapter. I want you to track your money. The longer you can track it, the better. Track it to the penny. Find out exactly what you are doing with your money and how you are handling it. You are addressing your mindset, which is top priority, so now you need to see what you really do with your money. This is how you begin to rewire the mind. You take the keys to your damn life back. You become EMPOWERED. You stop letting money control you, and you take control of it. You say no more to living in a survival mindset, and you get to work.

Track your money for at least two weeks. If you can track longer, then do it. One full month will give you solid data to examine. After you track your money, I want you to look at what you find. What are you spending your money on? Where can you scale back? Are you eating out all the time? Eating out is a big vice, and so is coffee. Do you have a retail addiction? We are addicted to the illusions of pleasures of life and, in turn, we suffer in lack, which denies us from living in our fullness. I am providing you with a space to track and to reflect on what you find. Don't do yourself an injustice by skipping this activity. No one is coming to save you. You can save yourself, but you must do the work that is required.

Date	Day of the week	Item(s) Purchased	Amount

Date	Day of the week	Item(s) Purchased	Amount

Date	Day of the week	Item(s) Purchased	Amount

Now that your tracking time has come to a close, I want you to reflect and examine how you spend your money. How well do you spend money? Did you have things coming out of your account that you didn't know about? Do you eat out every day, and is it adding up? Do you have a habit that is consuming a nice chunk of change? What did you discover from tracking your money? What did you learn? Reflect on everything and then create some money goals—some savings goals. Make a plan on how you will manage your money better. How are you going to be EMPOWERED with the way you handle your money? Use the space provided to write.

_____

_____

_____

_____

_____

_____

_____

_____

_____

_____

_____

_____

_____

_____

_____

_____

_____

"The secret to creating lasting financial change is to decide to pay yourself first and then make it automatic."

—David Bach, author and entrepreneur

How do you start paying yourself? You just do it. I want you to take your next paycheck and start with 1% or 5% and save it. You can start with a basic savings account. I suggest opening one that you don't need a debit card for, one where you must walk into the bank to withdraw money. This will help you in the long run. Why? Because you'll have to think just a bit longer before you pull the money out. You are going to need to be emotionally intelligent with your money and understand you must delay gratification. I am going to dive deeper regarding emotional intelligence and delayed gratification in the chapters ahead. For now, I just need you to say no to eating out so damn much and buying all that coffee and say yes to your savings so you can begin to shift the narrative of your financial mind. I also want you to stop doing so much for others and start doing more for yourself.

Once you begin to rewire your mind and write the new narrative, I want you to pursue unto death the building of generational wealth. We don't stay on this earth, you understand. Every last one of us will depart, and the legacy we leave is imperative to future generations. As the chosen generational curse breakers and generational blessing makers, it is up to us to build the empire that is set to change the future generations. I am building for 100 generations, if not more. I know I look insane on all levels of my mansion, but I have the Willy Wonka of all elevators. Do you want to get in? I bet you do. I am living the Empowered Life, and so can you!

TWO

"It is very important to understand that emotional intelligence is not the opposite of intelligence, it is not the triumph of heart over head—it is the unique intersection of both."

—David Caruso, actor

Wounded emotion will win time and time again against logic. Even though your logic is undeniable, it doesn't, nor will it ever, matter to wounded emotion. Emotional Intelligence (EI or EQ), on the other hand, will always give way to logic, and it holds great space for emotion but doesn't allow you to stay trapped in emotion. You must exchange your wounded emotion for EQ. When you do, you will be mentally and emotionally stronger—and a much healthier person overall.

How do you do that, you may ask? First, you must acknowledge that you need help. That you, too, like everyone else on this crazy place called earth, have some issues that need to be dealt with and you refuse to die with them. You then reach out and find some therapy and pursue self-awareness, personal development, and knowledge like they're a billion dollars just waiting to be had.

Secondly, find help. There are many resources out there for you. You can do a Google search and come up with a thousand and one resources. In the Introduction, I shared the therapies I swear by. For me personally, they have been lifesaving. Talk therapy is a wonderful place to start, but if you have experienced anywhere near what I have, then you will need to move from talk therapy to a more action-based therapy. We have a trauma body, and the body keeps score. In order to truly be free from the trauma, we must do the work required to pull it off our body. We start by saying, "*I am done carrying this weight, this shame. I am tired of dancing with wounded emotion, and I deserve to be emotionally intelligent.*"

Self-awareness is key to living the Empowered Life. The more self-aware we are, the better we are at managing our life and all that comes our way. EQ goes hand in hand with self-awareness. EQ is the ability to understand your emotions, to understand why you do what you do, and to learn how to control your responses to triggers and the waves of life. There are so many layers of programming that we will work to pull off of us in our lifetime. As you do the work required to heal yourself, you will find a better understanding of who you truly are. Because we can be trapped in wounded emotion and actually function there, we must learn to deactivate that programming first. We do that by consistently working through our trauma under the care of a therapist. We do that by reading books about healing, emotional intelligence, and the like. We do that by holding space for our self, knowing that we are a work in progress. We may forever be a work in progress, but with each day, we do get better if we don't give up.

There are many different personality assessments on the market, and you may have taken some in the past, but there is one I would like to introduce to you—one that I took myself. The 4 Animals is an assessment that combines about five different evaluations. What I love about this assessment is that it indicates what your natural side is, and what your adaptable side is. I am always so fascinated by the psychology of why we do what we do, especially when we get around others. As you grow in self-awareness, you are growing in the knowledge of your personal psyche. You are pulling back the layers of your mind and exposing the subconscious. This work is so important not only to living the Empowered Life, but also to awakening to a greater level of consciousness.

"Clearly, then, the city is not a concrete jungle, it is a human zoo."

—Desmond Morris, author and scientist

Let us now meet the four animals. There is a lion, and I am 99% lion. We run this jungle. At least, we think we do. We are results-driven. Did you know that a lion is only awake four hours out of the day? However, what they get done in those four hours is enough to let everyone in the jungle know they are in charge. The same is true with human Lions. We execute and do so at a very high level. What it takes someone else to do in an eight-hour day we finish in four.

The next animal I would like for you to meet is the very flashy, ever so beautiful, never shuts up, and doesn't like to be alone, flamingo. I am also 74% flamingo. They are the hostess with the mostest and will make anyone feel right at home. Very social, the flamingo's strengths are by far its ability to communicate, but they can go on for long periods of time if not constrained. They do make some of the best conversationalists, and you are sure to enjoy the company of a flamingo.

Next, I would like to introduce you to the chameleon. What is the first thing that comes to mind when you think of the word chameleon? One of the first things most people think of is adaptability, or the ability to change color and blend in. Indeed, the chameleon is one of the best supporters around because they will adapt to their environment. That is until they feel the need to go support someone else. Then they can be called shady—no pun intended. Oftentimes, chameleons are suffering in silence. They struggle with making a decision. They don't want to hurt anyone, but many times end up hurting themselves. They can feel torn and be pulled at from too many directions. This can make it difficult for them to function. They simply want to see that everyone makes it to shore safely. I have very little chameleon, which shocks me because I feel like, especially with my homeless work, I don't want anyone to be left behind. However, my lion is so dominant that it waits on no one. The ship is leaving, regardless if you made it on or not. We out.

The fourth and final animal I would like to introduce you to is the turtle. Everyone needs a turtle on their team. They are the ones with all the details. They are going to be cautious and careful with just about everything. They, however, can get in their own way by trying to get everything in order. They are very slow to execute because they are carefully checking things out from all angles. They are big on systems and are wonderful planners. However, if something doesn't go to plan, they can be thrown off. I have almost no turtle. But I promise you, when I do use my tiny percent of turtle, I am a damn Mutant Ninja Turtle. Watch out!

These are your four animals, and each of them resides in us but at different levels. The superpower is in the fact that you do have all four animals. Learning to master them is the key. It is my lion that has saved me time and time again due to my intense and tragic backstory. I could not have grown my business the way I did without my lion. I can attest I move quickly and need to hurry up and slow down. I need to activate turtle power and pull out more details. Just wait a few moments longer, then attack. I have never been big on assessments because I am an anomaly and I just can't be put in a box. But I love the 4 Animals, and today I teach all my students about it. I also share it with my clients. I do workshops just on them, and it is an entire jungle experience.

Because this assessment indicates your natural side and your adaptable side, you are able to better understand why you do what you do. For example, I am 99% lion naturally, but when I first took the assessment, my adaptable lion was only 47 percent. When I saw that, I was taken aback. I thought to myself, *Why is my adaptable lion so low? What is going on?* Then I realized I hide. I used to hide a lot. I hid behind my hair. Let me cover my face, and you won't see how fat it is. I hid behind my education. See how smart I am, but don't you dare look at me because if you do, you'll see a broken soul. The list of things I used to hide behind goes on and on. I was hiding because I had been abused for so long that I had no true confidence in the beauty of my authentic self. It was not until I began doing the work required to heal myself that I began to love myself. It took a lot of work to get where I am today, and I am still working on my healing because I refuse to die with the demons. In this life, you must do the work to heal yourself. I believe in personal development and growth, both of which are required to live the Empowered Life.

Once I realized I was hiding my beautiful lion, I was able to work on not hiding her. You see, as I stated earlier, it is because of her that I made it through. It was because of her drive that I was able to build my businesses. It is because of her that I was able to never give up. It is because of her that I have the strength to build my greatest empire yet. I am done hiding my beauty because it intimidates others. That is no longer my concern. I was made to shine and shine I will. I was made to roar and roar I will. I was made to execute and execute I will. What have you been made to do that you are hiding? I want you to stop hiding your beautiful, authentic self. I want you to own your amazingness. I want you to know that because I was able to see that I had been hiding my beautiful lion, I began working on changing that. I took the assessment a year later, and wouldn't you know it, my adaptable lion had risen. I was no longer hiding the beauty in the beast.

The four animals are the strength in my superpowers. I am learning to master each of them to make me a better leader, educator, servant, friend, and parent. I encourage you to take the assessment, which only takes about five minutes. You get a 22-page report that is extremely valuable to self-awareness and personal development. Specifically, there a section on how to communicate effectively with other animals and how you like to be communicated with. This is golden. Just like finding out what your love language is, finding out how you communicate and how you prefer to be spoken to is vital to living a more Empowered Life. You may contact me directly to take the assessment. I do sell them, along with a personal deep dive of the report and how to effectively dominate the jungle you live in by using all four animals. The way out is within. The deeper you crawl within and heal, the freer you will become. Life is short. How much time has already been lost? Too much, I say, and that ends now.

I need you to understand how you work and get to know yourself better. I need you to understand agreements that you have that are truly yours, and those that are programmed in you. Yes, every human being has been programmed. I need you to find out your programming and decide if you truly agree with all that your programming indicates you are. How we see ourselves is directly related to how we will lead our lives. If you believe that your talents are set in stone, then you will stay stuck. You will keep repeating one hell of a rollercoaster ride by trying to prove yourself over and over again. You will stay in the valley of validation when you simply need to walk in the victory of being your authentic self. Stop wasting time trying to prove how great you are. Try to grow and get better.

"No matter what, people grow. If you chose not to grow, you're staying in a small box with a small mindset. People who win go outside of that box. It's very simple when you look at it."

—Kevin Hart, comedian and actor

Mindset is instrumental to living the Empowered Life. There are two types of mindsets: fixed and growth. The fixed mindset is very constraining and keeps us bound. The growth mindset, on the other hand, is very liberating. The fixed mindset believes that talent and intelligence are all that's needed to be successful. The fixed mindset doesn't take well to criticism or failure and normally only sees one way. The growth mindset believes that talent and intelligence, combined with hard work, will win every time. Even in failure, the growth mindset sees a winning score. The growth mindset is a lifelong learner and never turns down an opportunity to better oneself. The growth mindset understands the importance of practice and the dedication to pursuing goals. The growth mindset goes through setbacks with an innate ability to persevere. The growth mindset is gritty. The higher your EQ, the more of a growth mindset you have.

The rewiring of the mind and our emotional state takes time. It helps that our brains have neuroplasticity, which means we have the ability to form new neural connections. The more time and effort we spend on something, the more we build a pathway in our brains for it. This is how the growth mindset works. We are not fixed in place. We can learn more, and we can change our way of thinking. But we must be deliberate and intentional. We must do the daily work required to set a new pathway in our mind until it becomes second nature.

I want you to see yourself as a farmer. You just received a plot of land. Right now, it has lots of overgrown shrubs, thistles, and animals running wild. But you have eyes to see beyond that. Not only do you have sight beyond what you see in the natural world, but you also are not afraid of the work that is required to create it as you see it in your mind's eye. You begin to work your land. Slow and steady wins the race, my dear one. It will not be a quick fix that brings the clearing of the land. Oh no, it will require hard work. It will require early mornings and late nights. It will require a confidence in self like never before. It will require discipline. But before you know it, not only will you have cleared the land of all that kept it in a decrepit state, but you'll have built a house to live in, and your land will bear fruit and flourish with abundance. This is the work we need to do with our minds. EQ, a growth mindset, and grit are essential tools you will need to be a successful farmer. In the next chapter, I am going to dive deeper into grit. But before we leave this chapter, I am going to give you one more tool that goes hand in hand with EQ: delayed gratification.

One of my favorite emotional intelligence experts is Ashley Zahabian. She discovered EQ through her own struggle with severe anorexia. Today, she is one of the most powerful speakers and leadership experts in the world. One of the elements of EQ that she really goes into is delayed gratification. What is delayed gratification? It is waiting for something better. Saying "no" now because your "YES" is so much better. Saying, *"No, I am not taking the weekend getaway because I want to take the trip to Rome later this year. The weekend getaway money will now go into the Rome account."* It means going to the gym today and every day, staying consistent because you know that the results will come. It means that when you are paying yourself first, you take that money and save it for later. You deny yourself right now because your gratification for what is to come is so much better. It takes patience, emotional control and regulation, and effective self-leadership.

To change takes work. The work can be painful to do. This is why many people stay in a place of dysfunction. Functional as they may be, they are hurting inside, and the pain eventually oozes out. They are not able to truly control their emotions because they are wounded, and as I stated at the beginning of this chapter, wounded emotion will never allow logic to win. This is why we must be intentional about turning our wounded emotion into emotional intelligence. We are energy, yes? We are in **motion**, yes? We are e-motion, and we should honor that emotion. It is a beautiful piece of our humanity.

"I truly believe in positive synergy, that your positive mindset gives you a more hopeful outlook, and belief that you can do something great means you will do something great."

—Russell Wilson, American athlete

You are going to do great things in this life. Far greater than you could imagine. You have been called to live the Empowered Life. The keys to your life are in your hands now. Take some time to reflect on what we have covered in this chapter. Where do you see yourself having a fixed mindset? Where do some of your wounded emotions hide? What goals can you put in place to begin plowing your land? You are the farmer. This is your life. *The way out is within.* Space is provided to write, and remember, just allow what comes to come. Do not hinder it. Freely write and allow your soul to speak to you. I also want you to do additional research on emotional intelligence. I want you to learn as much about as you possibly can. It will add to your life, and it is yet another key.

THREE

"Grit is passion and perseverance for long-term and meaningful goals."

—Angela Duckworth, author and psychologist

One of the best compliments I have ever received was when someone told me I was gritty. Now, mind you, I had no clue what the hell that meant at first. I was like, *"Huh, I have grit in my teeth?"* *(SMILE.)* But then the granter of such a wonderful compliment went on to tell me what grit was. Then he proceeded to tell me, "Stay gritty, baby," and that is exactly what I did and will continue to do. I don't know about you, but I am a person of passion. It flows from my toes to the crown of my head. My passion has been met in the past with pretty high emotion. But remember, I have exchanged my wounded emotion for emotional intelligence, and by doing so, I have better control. This control allows me to be directional with my passion. I am committed. This is very important to living the Empowered Life. Many people are interested in things like writing a book or losing weight or starting a business or whatever the case may be. The question is: Are you ready to do the work that is required? *Sure, let's go.*

Well, the first step you need to do is move past being interested and become committed. Why? Those who are only interested will do minimal work, but those who are committed will do whatever it takes. Very few people move past their interest in things. This is why they start things and don't finish them. They simply lose interest. They don't like some of the more boring aspects of the work that is required. Or they don't like how intense the pressure becomes when the work level increases. Gritty people, on the other hand, say, "Bring it on. I am made for this." Gritty people understand that it is not how smart they are nor how talented they are, but rather their ability to stay in the game. They play the long game, not the short game. This is the game of life. And if you are going to live the Empowered Life, you must master it.

"Resilience is not what happens to you. It's how you react to, respond to, and recover from what happens to you."

—Jeffrey Gitomer, author

Resilience and grit are tied together in a beautifully colored bow—the sparkly silver kind with splashes of many colors. You know, the ones when the light hits them just right and a rainbow appears. This, to me, is the bow of resilience and grit. I am always amazed at just how resilient we are as humans. We have the ability to bounce back. I know for me, I have been through the depths of suffering and pain. But yet, I still stand before you in my right mind on most good days, and I still have the courage to live out loud and continue to pursue my wildest dreams.

Now let me break down this bow to you a little more. Those sparkles of many colors, those are all the pieces of hell I have been through. When the light hits them just right, they sparkle. But the way they sparkle is the base of that silver. That silver base is my grit. I am not afraid of the suffering. I am not afraid of the pain. I had to endure it, and you have to endure yours. Resilience is your ability to endure. When you endure, you pull through and come out the other side stronger, and you shine a little brighter. You are determined to see the dreams you have inside you become a reality. You begin working, and you don't give a damn how long it takes or what obstacles get in your way, you are going to make it. Just watch and see. You are gritty, and there is no other way to be.

The silver grit, to me, represents STEEL, which is my legacy. You see, I was purposed to be born, abused, withstand, and overcome in this life because I am here to Serve, Teach, Encourage, Empower, and Lead. I am the STEEL Legacy. I have been operating under the STEEL Legacy for sixteen years with the work that I do for the homeless. I am now starting to legally form it into a nonprofit, out of which I plan to build a very powerful organization that is going to have an even greater impact than I have seen to date. This is how we change the narrative. We take possession of our story. We own what happened to us, and we showcase it as the colorful coat that it really is. Like the coat of many colors from the story of Joseph in the Bible, we wear it proudly. Then, we use it to help others heal and be free.

You have been chosen in this lifetime to heal so that you can help those who come after you to live in the light. This doesn't mean you will not live in the light, oh no, dear one. You are the light. That's just it. You are a star holder. I will share the story of the star with you in just a few chapters. For now, just know not to let anyone dull your sparkle. Shine brightly. And remember, God works all things to His good.

Let us now reflect. I want you to have a moment of time where you think about all you have endured thus far. Take a moment to reflect and write what comes. It may hurt a little. I encourage your tears to flow. I encourage you to allow whatever to come, come, and don't stop it. No more stuffing it down. No more suffocating the truth. No more shame in your story. Reflect and write. Then, I want you to think about how gritty you are. Do you start and stop projects? If you do, that is okay, because now you are going to work on changing that learned behavior. You are going to remove limitations that keep you from committing to you—committing to what you really want to see happen in your life.

If you know you are a gritty person, then I am going to challenge you to get a little grittier. I want you to get a little bolder. I want you to dream just a little bigger. As big of a dreamer and doer as I am, I still come under. The Bible tells me that He will bless me far more abundantly, and beyond all I could ask for or imagine. This is why I know I still play it small and come under. I am not only challenging you, but I am also challenging myself. I am tired of us not having what belongs to us by divine order and our natural birthright. I encourage you to be tired too. Not tired to where you want to give up—oh no, tired to the point where you realize you have had enough. You don't see the change in the world, so you are going to be the change. The way out is within. Now go within and write what comes.

_____

_____

There really is no finish line, you see. Goals are achieved, and new ones are set. I like to say old ceilings become new floors because that is what happens when we live the Empowered Life. We set goals, we accomplish them, and then we move on to our next set of goals. We know that no matter what, if we just keep pressing forward, we will see our dreams come to pass.

I pursued my MBA (**M**aster's in **B**usiness **A**dministration) not only to become a better businesswoman, but also to be able to teach at the community college. I graduated in 2010, and I didn't get my first college teaching job until 2015. I pursued the college professor goal for five years. Along the journey, there were many steps I had to take. I need you to understand the importance of steps and how they play in to being gritty. Every step is important. Next level steps are required. If you miss a step, you are missing a very important piece of the puzzle. Steps require patience, not talent or smarts. This is why it is so important to be gritty. Gritty people don't give up, no matter how long it takes.

It took me over a year to lose that hundred pounds. That, my friends, is a lot of weight to carry, and a lot of weight to get rid of. I had to use a lot of self-denial and delayed gratification. Every day, I had to stick with my meal prep, my workout regimen, and my mental health. As I shared before, with health and with life, it boils down to a formula: 80% mental, 19% food, and 1% workout. I had to be mentally strong. Being emotionally intelligent helped me be mentally strong. I had to prep my food and eat it daily. I had to drink my water and a lot of it. I had to say "no" to many things, including people. Those were all steps—next level steps. Then, after a little over a year, I went from a size 24 to a size 8, and from just under 300 pounds to 179 pounds.

I promise I am gritty and pretty supernatural at times. But I am also subject to being a human and encountering setbacks. As I told you all in the introduction, I slowly gained some weight back. I stopped being as committed as I was. I went to just being interested in eating right. Interest fades, and when you are only interested and not fully committed, you do very little. I lost my discipline. Something even deeper happened, however. A piece of unresolved trauma started to come to the surface. Shame of my body. Shame of how I looked. Shame, shame, I know your name.

"Being gritty doesn't mean not showing pain or pretending everything is O.K. In fact, when you look at healthy and successful and giving people, they are extraordinarily meta-cognitive. They're able to say things like, 'Dude, I totally lost my temper this morning.' That ability to reflect on yourself is signature to grit."

—Angela Duckworth, author and psychologist

I reflected, and I knew I needed help. I knew I needed to go back to therapy. And that is what I did. I knew that if I was going to kill this demon once and for all, I needed to go back and keep digging up what was still there. Talk about tired. I have found myself many times over tired of doing therapy. I thought to myself, *How much longer do I need to do this? How much more do I need to throw up? Haven't I thrown up enough already?* I want you to understand something: if you are going to fully be free of what you have endured in this life, you are going to need to do intense mental health work. This is not just my opinion; this is clinical. This is fact-based. But as a living witness, I can testify that it wasn't until I started doing EMDR therapy that I began to start to lift from the prison I was in. It is not a quick process. It is going to require a tremendous amount of effort on your part. You are probably going to have the urge time and time again to stop because of reliving the pain. You are going to get physically sick as the trauma begins to release from your body. You are going to shift in your life, and people, places, and things will begin to drift away. And they must, because if they don't, you will not heal.

My abuse was just the beginning. Then I suffered from side effects, which not only kept me imprisoned for even longer, but also caused me more trauma. I will probably throw up for several more years—even though, at this point, I have been throwing up for a full decade. What I won't be doing is throwing up my entire life. Nor will I suffer in silence and operate out of a wounded spirit. No, I am the STEEL Legacy and the most beautiful silver bow you have ever seen—the kind with many colors when the light hits it just right. And if you look close enough, you will see me holding my star.

You will need to be gritty your entire life. Yes, even unto death. Gritty people have hope; they are optimistic about the future. To understand and have hope for eternal life means you will stay gritty until the day you die. You will never lose your passion and your perseverance for the long-term goal to live forever—unless you don't want to live forever, whatever the hell that looks like. But I do! And the way I plan to do that in the land of the living is with the Eternal Enterprise, which is my publishing company. Words are eternal. My words now make me immortal. My story and your story, they are powerful. But they die with you if you don't share them. Maybe you are not ready to share your story. That is okay. Maybe you don't ever want to share your story with the public like I do. That is okay, too. But I do encourage you to write. That is why I have given you space to do so in this book and will continue to do so. In the final chapter, I will give you one final challenge, and I pray you will do it. It is for your legacy. But for now, I need you to do one thing for me: I need you to stay gritty, baby. You are learning to live the Empowered Life. This is a long game, and you are going to master it.

FOUR

"Greatness is more than potential. It is the execution of that potential. Beyond the raw talent. You need the appropriate training. You need the discipline. You need the inspiration. You need the drive."

—Eric A. Burns, author and playwright

Y ou will get nowhere fast if you fail to execute. The reason I have been so successful and will continue to be successful is because I am a LION. I am results-oriented. I execute. What does execution look like? It looks like getting off your ass and getting to work. You can't just sit there, look at the plan you wrote, say, "Hey, that looks great," and marvel at the way you were able to put some words on paper. That will never generate you one dime, nor will it add anything to your life. You must be disciplined and proactive. Execution often requires you to change your behavior. If you plan to achieve something you have never achieved before, you must do things you have never done. That takes a change in your behavior, and your mindset must be up to the challenge.

Another reason why people are often unable to execute is because they are trying to do too many things. You must narrow your focus. You need to stop multitasking. That only trains your brain to procrastinate. Multitasking is an illusion, as the brain only can work on one thing at a time. Your mental strength is everything when it comes to execution. To train your brain successfully, you need to learn to complete one project at a time. Treat your mind like a muscle. It takes time to build up muscle by going to the gym, lifting weights, and eating right. The same is true for your mind. Any weightlifter will tell you that you don't lift your arm weights and press legs at the same time. You do one exercise at a time. You do that with pure focus, deliberate practice, and repetition.

"Infuse your life with action. Don't wait for it to happen. Make it happen. Make your own future. Make your own hope. Make your own love."

—Bradley Whitford, actor

If you are truly going to live the Empowered Life, you will need to become strategic with your life goals, your career goals, and your legacy goals—all of which tie together. I want you to start by thinking about your legacy goals. What kind of legacy do you want to leave? Each one of us must transcend. We leave behind everything and only take the love with us. So, what do you do want to leave behind? For me, personally, not only do I plan to leave generational wealth, but I will also be leaving the blessings of healing, strength, and humanitarianism. The only way to leave such things is by creating the life of those things. We lead by example. We also leave the example, and we trust that our seeds will do right by that example.

I am building for a hundred generations, if not more. I will be leaving writings of magnitude for my seeds. Wisdom and guiding principles that I pray and truly believe will be used by them in their lives. I will leave blueprints on how to play the game of life and win by serving others without losing self. Because I have been chosen in this lifetime to be a generational curse breaker and generational blessing maker, my seeds are already set to walk in the blessings. This doesn't mean life will be easy. Oh no, on the contrary, I imagine that they will be fighting a battle much larger than the ones we currently fight. However, they will be much better equipped because of the work I have done. You see, they need me to break the chain so that they may set the captives free. I am not only setting people free today, I am setting them free for hundreds of years to come. You want to know how? My legacy. My seeds. My seeds upon seeds and so on. This is the calling. I believe that this, too, is your calling.

There are many generational curses out there. In just a bit, I will ask you to give some thought to the ones that are specific to your family tree and must be broken for not only you but your legacy. I do want to share one of the things that I believe is the most damaging in our world by far: it is the heart. You see, our heart is extremely powerful, far more powerful than we give it credit for. But in our country, people are dying at rapid speed due to heart conditions. This is not a physical element as much as it is a spiritual element. People's hearts are broken. People's hearts are cold and blocked from receiving love. People's hearts are hurting deeply. Trauma has a direct effect on the heart. For me personally, I had a block over my heart that would not allow me to hear any good about myself. It was a defense mechanism, but it was being used against me. Imagine that! Something that I thought was protecting me was actually keeping me sick. With the help of my therapist and the use of EMDR, I was able to do the work needed to free my heart.

The work I did was action-oriented. I had to execute. I had to not only do work in the therapy room but also outside. Upon the discovery of this block over my heart, my therapist asked me to find something in the room that represented what I was feeling. In addition to doing EMDR, she also did sand tray therapy and art therapy. She had an entire bookcase full of different trinkets that she used for the sand tray therapy. It was there that I found a beautiful crystal desk clock. The time was frozen on the clock. Funny how that ties in. I think we often feel frozen when our abuse happens. We keep growing physically, yes, but there is still a piece of us frozen in time, trapped and suffering. This clock was so heavy. I thought, *Yes, this is it! This is what is covering my heart.* She told me to keep the clock, take it home, set it on my desk, and just meditate on it as often as I could. I would also bring it back in with me during our future sessions. In the process of working with this clock, I discovered many things.

First, I really wanted to get the time working. I thought that would help me a lot just to get the time moving again. I didn't want to be frozen in a place of suffering. So, one day I decided to take the timepiece off the body and get it fixed. A new battery was all it needed. A new battery was inside, and the time began to tick away. Then, shortly after, it stopped, and I couldn't get it started again. In this first act, I was trying to jump to the end. I was trying to skip steps, which, as I already shared, next level steps were required. I had much more work to do. Because I am a LION, I want to move fast. This part of me can be challenging to deal with, and maybe you, too, would like to get right to the result. But there is a process to everything. There are critical steps that must be done in order to get the results we are looking for, the ones that will actually last. I had to hurry up and slow down.

I decided I needed to turn my attention to the body itself. It was so heavy. So was the covering over my heart. I was in need of a breakthrough. I worked with the clock for a long time. Years. This is important. It takes time to pull trauma off you. Even the smallest step in the right direction will get you to where you are going as long as you keep moving forward. Finally, I was ready to break the clock. I was done with the weight of carrying it over my heart. I had already separated the timepiece from the body and kept them separate, but the weight needed to go. Mother's Day 2017, I took that crystal body and I beat the shit out of it. It was not easy to break it up, but I just kept beating it and beating it over and over. It began to break apart. Then, before you knew it, there, in what seemed like a million pieces, was the body of a beautiful crystal clock that had kept me a prisoner for decades. I did it. I broke through.

All the steps I had done over the years brought me to one very big moment: my heart was now fully free to feel. I took a few remains of the clock body and put them in a bag and tied them to about a dozen balloons. Then I released the balloons, which is one of my favorite things to do. I did this with my children by my side. I cried like a baby as I watched the balloons disappear into the sky, taking years of my abuse with them. In that moment, I received beauty for ashes. And so did my children. You see, I am not doing this without them. This life I am doing with my children. They are directly affected by my lead, so it is important I lead them correctly. The greatest gift I could possibly give them outside of the knowledge of the Lord and the eternal love of God is the healing of myself. Breaking the curse off my life. Planting the blessing. By the time I had released the clock body, I had also released 100 pounds. The work I had done along the way gave me the results I was looking for. If I had just written the plan down but never did the work that was required, I would still be suffering in silence, and the clock would still be covering my heart.

Now, to tie this in a bit more as it relates to generational curses, my family has a history of heart issues. From my grandmother to my aunts to my cousins. Many of them—well, almost all of them—suffer from some type of heart issue. Again, this is trauma—a deep history of ancestral curses. But on Mother's Day 2017, a dozen balloons lifted into the sky with a bag attached to them that held pieces of a broken curse, and, as it drifted away, so did its attachment to me and my seeds upon seeds.

I want you to think about the generational curses that plague your family, the ones that have kept you enslaved. I want you to use the space provided to write what comes to you. Then I want you to decide right here and now that you are going to break those curses. You are going to pursue unto death the mission of being the generational curse breaker and blessing maker. You must remember that execution will always be required to not only break the curse but to plant the blessing. Therefore, after you write what those curses are, I want you to list the blessings you want to leave behind. I want you to take one curse and start with that curse. You are going to write steps, action-oriented steps that you are going to take in order to break the curse. Perhaps the first step is to get help. As I have encouraged you in the past, EMDR therapy is one of the best action-oriented therapies around. It works. But you must be willing to work it.

_____

_____

_____

_____

_____

_____

_____

_____

_____

_____

_____

_____

_____

_____

_____

"It's really amazing to stand in front of a work you haven't seen before and be almost overwhelmed by its beauty and the vision and execution of the artist."

—Paul Allen, American business magnate

One day, the work of your life will be seen by those who have yet to come. They will stand before your work, and, just as the above quote states, they will be overwhelmed by its beauty. This is why I work as hard as I do. This is why I say yes to call. This is why I write and speak. This is why I am on a mission to share the Empowered Life with everyone I can. I understand the importance of our work, our life, our legacy. I hope now that you spent some time thinking about your legacy, you have a little more fire burning within you to do what you need to do in order to make sure that what you have planned will come to pass.

I want to move us now from legacy to life. I want you to think about what some of your life goals are. We must first discover our life goals to then move us to our career goals. Reason being that your career is what is going to support your life. If you have life goals of traveling the world, then you are going to need either a career that allows you to do that, a significant other who can accommodate that, or one hell of a trust fund. Since we can't bank on the last two, let's go with the first option.

Take some time now to list some of your life goals. After you've identified what those are, I want you to list
some of your career goals. Then I need you to put some
actionable steps around each of them. I only want you to
work on one or two goals at a time. I want you to set
measurable and achievable milestones for yourself. I want
you to be honest with yourself, and if you are not doing
what you need to move yourself forward, I need you to get
it together. I need you to understand that no one is coming to save you. That is not how it works. No one is going
to walk up to you and give you the life goals you want, nor
the career you want. You must go get those for yourself.
You must execute. You must be intentional with what you
have set out to do. You must have emotional intelligence,
grit, and a drive to see the fruit of your work no matter
what. You may need to go without sleep some days to see
your dream come to pass. You may even have to go without food to see your dream come to pass. You may even
need to skip social outings to see your dream come to
pass. I can promise you it will all be worth it.

If you are as radical as I am, and you have a desire to
live an extraordinary life, you are going to have to do far
more than what average people do. You are going to have
to sacrifice in order to succeed. Take time now to write
what comes to you regarding your life and career goals.
Then, take one or two from each category and write out a
plan of action. Then, it's go time! Act on the plan. If you
don't, all you will have is words on paper. It will be of no

use to you, and the work that others are to be marveled by will be still locked inside you. You will have forfeited your keys to the Empowered Life. I cannot let that happen to you. You are reading this book on purpose, and I believe in you. I know you can do it. Now, write and get ready to do the work. You got this!

_____

_____

_____

_____

_____

_____

_____

_____

_____

_____

_____

_____

_____

_____

_____

_____

_____

_____

_____

FIVE

PALUMBO PRINCIPLE 6:
WE DON'T PREDICT OUR FUTURE,
WE CREATE IT

"The power for creating a better future is contained in the present moment: You create a good future by creating a good present."

—Eckhart Tolle, spiritual teacher

The sixth principle is one of my favorites because not only do I have the ability to be creative, I also have a vast imagination. I have vision for lifetimes. This is why I work as hard as I do. Faith is dead without works. And vision is intertwined with faith. Faith is seeing beyond what our natural eye can see. Remember the farmer in the last chapter? Being able to see an abundant promise land takes faith, especially when everything around looks far from anything promising. To live the Empowered Life, you are going to need to activate your ability to create. You will not be predicting; you are going to be a conscious creator. This chapter is going to give you some powerful tools to help you bring your vision to life. Don't miss one.

Prediction is unsure, but creation is a matter of fact. When you are creating, I want you to do more than just visualize. I want you to engage your senses. You see, when we bring the heart and the head together, there is nothing we cannot have or do. If you desire rain, don't just think about it and see it.... I need you to feel the rain on your face. I need you to smell the rain. I need you to walk around in your rain gear. This is how you activate a higher vibrational pull, and what you desire will come chasing after you. I have all kinds of vision boards—from poster boards to virtual ones that I keep on my phone. I am constantly making them. I put no time limit on the vision. Because, remember: though it may tarry, it is never late. It will be right on time. The vision is already ready. But it waits on you to be ready. It waits on divine alignment, which is exactly what you want it to do.

This book, and all the other books I write, start out on vision boards. The car I am currently driving was on a vision board. The money I am receiving from being a paid teacher is on a vision board. My wedding and marriage are on a vision board. I have one vision board manifesting at what seems to be the speed of light. So many things have all come to pass from this one vision board. What I can tell you is, I myself have become more aware of using my senses to feel my vision. This could very well be the reason this one board is appearing ever so quickly. That, and, well, I am ready. I am ready to receive what I desire.

Creating your future is not only possible for personal life, but for business life, as well. When I bought STFF, my core business, I was going to take over the US. I believe very much in active faith. I will buy or create things in pure faith. For my business, I created marketing materials that were magnets the shape of the US, with my logo and my name and contact information on them. I also had other fact sheets that I would send out to my clients and to potential clients, which also had the US on them. I was serious. I was coming for it. I didn't do too bad, truth be told. I captured 10% of the US. Imagine that—a welfare mom, who became the CEO of her own company, and who went on to capture 10% of the US. I did not predict that—nor could I—but I surely had the vision to create it.

I will still take the other 90% of the US, and I plan to capture the globe as well. Both the US and the globe are on several of my vision boards. I have seen myself traveling the world, speaking to seas upon seas of people, being the healer that I am. I know beyond a shadow of a doubt that I am the next top female speaker in the world, and soon to be an award-winning author. This, too, is on a vision board. It is not only on a vision board, but I see it and feel it with my senses. My heart and my mind are one. My vibrational level is elevated. I radiate at a high frequency, which draws to me what I desire.

You, too, can do the same. You must simply believe. You must remove the self-censor, which is in the center of your forehead. Do it now. Take your hand and place it on your forehead and grab it like you are going to pull your forehead off...but, please, don't do that—just play along. Grab your forehead and remove the self-censor. Just pull it off and throw that sucker away. Allow your creativity to take over. Believe in yourself and your vision. You don't need anyone else's approval to believe in yourself! And if you feel like you do need approval, you have just now been Professor Palumbo Approved! Boom!

I believe in this principle so much that I require all my students to create vision boards. I had one student tell me one time he thought vision boards were for thirteen-year-old girls. He was a bit resistant to it, but after he released his altered perspective, he began to really enjoy the process. I love receiving messages like that. It just proves that when you let go of limiting beliefs and thoughts, magic can happen. Another one of my favorite types of messages to receive is from those whose boards begin to bear fruit. Those messages are the most powerful ones, and they make my heart leap.

There is no limit to the number of boards you can create. As I stated, I have tons of them. And at the drop of a hat, I will take my phone and get to creating. I collect pictures and place them in a beautiful collage, and then I spend time meditating on them. Experiencing them. Bringing them into the now. Activating my senses. Because then it becomes real. We don't just have memories of the past; we have future memories, too. The more I awaken, the more I realize the truth behind quantum physics and the supernatural. Come dance with me for just a moment as I share some of the depths of truth that reside in our world.

We are always in the now. That is the only door open. The past door is locked. The future door is locked. I need you to stop wasting your only open door by beating on doors that are closed. I need you to learn how to heal from the door of the past and be free from it. This takes work. It takes therapy such as EMDR, which activates past memories that you bring into the now. You then work through those memories and heal from them. The future is also locked, but in moments of stillness, in moments of elevation, you lift from the now and enter a different realm. It takes time to master this. The more you practice it, the stronger you will become. Eventually, you will transcend to teacher. And teach, you must!

Let's dive deeper into the now. You catch a plane in San Francisco that takes you to Chicago, then on to London, finally landing in Africa. You never leave the plane. You start in one place but end up in another place. This, my dear one, is life. The entire plane ride, you are in the now. There really is no yesterday, nor is there a tomorrow. The now is the plane. You cannot leave the plane until you arrive at your destination. Along the plane ride, turbulence takes place. This turbulence scares you because it is lasting too long. This doesn't seem normal. You call the flight attendant over. You express your concern. He or she tells you that there is an empty seat under the wing. Turbulence is usually not as bad under the wing. But you cannot get off the plane. You move and sit under the wing. And, indeed, the turbulence settles a bit. But you can still feel it.

"He shall cover you with His feathers, and under His wings shall you trust; His truth shall be your shield and buckler."

—Psalms 91:4

The turbulence of life comes, and we cannot get off the plane. We don't leave the now—not in physical form, at least. But we can sit under the wing. Even then, we must trust. We must hold faith that the turbulence will subside. As you call the flight attendant over another time to address the concern of the turbulence, he or she tells you not to worry, the pilot is going to take us to a higher elevation, and the turbulence will fade. Your response needs to be THANK YOU because gratitude opens the door to the now that already exists. If you recall in Chapter One, I explained that I no longer ask for abundance; I give thanks for it. I give thanks for not only my abundance, but my vision. I give thanks for the turbulence and all the suffering I have endured. It has given me a story to share. It has given me the power to inspire others and help them break free.

Right now, I want you to say THANK YOU. Thank you first to yourself for all you have endured in this life to date. I want you to say thank you for all you desire to have. Give thanks for your life right now. Rejoice. You have been chosen to be here in the NOW. Stop wasting time knocking like a crazy person on a door you'll never be able to open. Raise your frequency by accessing a greater level of emotional intelligence. Awaken to the power of the NOW, and in that place, I want you to create. The creator has endowed you with everything you need. Granted, you may be picking things up along the way, but the creator has already laid them out for you. We must learn to make the most of the present. Only the human possesses the now. Spirit is infinite and eternal. But we are carnal, with a body of flesh that resides in the now. We do have power, however, to access what is already ours. We do this by mediation. We do this by activating a vibrational level that is found above the turbulence. It is done with a grateful heart.

When you create your vision boards, I want you to sit with them in a state of meditation. I want you to use your senses and truly experience things on a 3-dimensional level. Bring it to life. What you are doing in that moment is bringing future into the now. Then nothing will stop you from having it. Why? Because you already experienced it. You know, without question, that it is going to take place. You are free to surrender because you trust in what you have not only seen, but what you experienced. You brought the future into the now, which is the only thing a carinal body has access to. Now, you can move forward and do the uncommon because no longer are you bound by limitations. You are enlightened, and you are living the Empowered Life.

"Music gives a soul to the universe, wings to the mind, flight to the imagination, and life to everything."

—Plato, Greek philosopher

Music has the ability to evoke emotion and memories. There is great power in music, and we love to watch a good movie. Movies have a way of drawing us in, making us feel like we are a part of the story. One minute we are rolling on the floor in laughter, and the next, we are on the edge of our seat in suspense. I am now going to share another way you can create vision: by using what is called a mind movie. The concept was created by Dr. Joe Dispenza, a well-known bestselling author and educator. A mind movie is essentially your vision in motion—a mini movie of your future with a soundtrack. A very simple way to create one is to find pictures on your phone using Google. Save those pictures to your camera roll. Then, using a movie creator application such as InShot, you can place the pictures into a movie and find music that inspires you, then add it over your movie. You can do the same process using your computer or laptop. You have now created your own personal mini movie of your future.

Here is one more important key that you will need to add to your mind movie: a kaleidoscope. You can find different types of kaleidoscope videos on YouTube. The kaleidoscope activates the mind and sets it in a transcendental state. This state is a perfect breeding ground for creation. You will want to place your kaleidoscope at the beginning of your movie. It is up to you how long you'd like it to run. I recommend trying 60– 90 seconds, then cut to your pictures. I also suggest having different music for your kaleidoscope part. Soft meditation music—something light like this will help the activation of your brain. Then, when your pictures start, shift your music. The best times to watch the movie are in the morning right upon waking and in the evening right before you drift off to sleep. Remember that while you are watching your movie, you will need to experience it as if it is already happening. Using your senses, I need you to see it in the now.

I highly recommend you research Dr. Joe Dispenza and learn more about the powerful work he does. The mind movies are tools he uses in his workshop around the world. It is also noted in his book, *Becoming Supernatural: How Common People Are Doing the Uncommon*, that the mind movies are being used with youth to help them create a vision for themselves. Our youth today are suffering from the demands of social media and the confines of their minds. The leading death of teens is suicide. This must stop. By creating a vision for their life using the mind movie tool, they can have hope for their future. They are able to open their heart to the possibilities of what they can and will achieve. As an educator who has worked with children and adults for many years, I can attest that we need more of this in our schools and in our world. We need to raise our frequency as a body of souls and activate a brighter future. It is available to us. We have a creator who loves us dearly. Our creator has bestowed upon us the ability to create, and it is up to us to do so. We don't have to play it small, either. Absolutely not!

"Now to Him who is able to do exceedingly abundantly above all that we ask or think, according to the power that works in us."

—Ephesians 3:20

Imagine, if you will for a moment, that all you created in your vision board and mind movie is only the surface of what you could achieve or have. I don't know about you, but I am floored. Why? Well, because I believe in some pretty radical things. I mean, come on, let's just start with the fact that I have already indicated to you I am building for 100 generations. Who does that? Where did that mindset come from? The above scripture, that's where. I believe in the Word. I believe that whatever it is I can imagine, my God tells me I could dream bigger! I know that I look insane to those whose narrative is still stuck in a world they never belonged to. This is why the commission on my life to go around and share the message of truth is so important, especially at this time in our history.

As I close this chapter, I am going to leave you with one last important key regarding the creation of your future: you must always speak life. The power of life and death is in the tongue. Our words have a frequency. The thoughts we have in our minds shape our world. This is why it is so important to capture those negative thoughts and throw them away, because they will fester and cause great damage if you don't. I suffered for many years with negative thoughts and a very hurtful voice. Even today, I am still not completely cured of those negative thoughts. But I am much more healed than I have ever been before. One thing for sure, I do the work that is needed to continue to pull layers of trauma off me. This is so important to understand. The work to be free is not going to be easy, but I can tell you it is so worth it. Please make sure you do the work you need to in order to set yourself free and ultimately change the direction of your entire family line.

You will need to silence the voice. You will need to change the narrative one line at a time. You have that power to create with word and with action. I am now going to leave you with space to write. I want you to come up with at least three to four different affirmations or positive statements regarding yourself and your life. Then I want you to meditate on them. I want you to speak them out loud. I want you to go to a mirror and look at your beautiful self and speak your life. Declare now that you are going to live the Empowered Life.

_____

_____

_____

_____

_____

_____

_____

_____

_____

_____

_____

_____

S I X

PALUMBO PRINCIPLE 5:
SACRIFICE TO SUCCEED

"The most important decision about your goals is not what you're willing to do to achieve them, but what you are willing to give up."

—Dave Ramsey, author and businessman

L iving the Empowered Life will consist of becoming successful. However, you will need to understand that in order to do so, you must sacrifice. You will have to sacrifice sleep, food, relationships, parties, events, movies, news events, family time, and the like. I can speak from experience and say this is what it will take for you to rise. You will make the sacrifice, and if you have a family, they will need to be aware that not only are you going to make sacrifices, but they will too. This can be the tricky part, especially for those of you who are married or have a significant other. If your spouse or partner is not on board with your vision and the direction you are going, you will need to figure out a way to get them on board. For your children, you will need to help them understand that the sacrifices will be well worth it in the end and that what you are doing is going to benefit them as well.

I am a firm believer in balance, so even though I have made many sacrifices, I have also made sure not to lose too much of myself and my time with my children. Everything else, however, I gave up. I don't watch TV. I don't even watch the news. (I do read, however, and I read a lot.) I don't go out to parties. When others are partying it up on Friday or Saturday nights, I am grinding or working out. I don't socialize, other than networking events to build my brand and business. I don't get caught up in family drama, and I have let go of several members of my family. I am a firm believer that "*family, friend, or foe—if they are toxic, you must let them go.*" Unfortunately, too many of my family members are toxic, so I gave myself the gift of goodbye. I did this with friendships and with my foes. So many people are afraid to be alone, but being with abusive people is much worse than being alone. You are going to have to make the sacrifice to let them go and trust your vision. Trust where you are going and the purpose of your life.

There are many sayings out there along the lines of, *you need to sacrifice like others will not in order to live like most never will.* This is so true. So many people will never even leave their backyard. Now, this isn't a bad thing if they are free and can take themselves to the ultra-limits while sitting in their backyard; for me, however, I could never just sit in my backyard. Nor would I. I can't sit still as it is, let alone in a yard. I need to be exposed to everything I possibly can. I desire to grow in culture and in character. I am planning for a hundred generations, if not more. In order to plan for that many generations, I must make sacrifices. I cannot play around like others do; I must be working. The grind never stops.

Emotional intelligence. Delayed gratification in action. This is what sacrificing to succeed really is all about. I want you to think for a moment or two on what you know you need to sacrifice right now in order to succeed. Are there people in your life you know you need to let go of? Are there some things in your life that need to go? Are there habits you have that need to go? In the space provided, I want you to list all that comes to mind regarding letting go and sacrificing. After you have made your list, I want you to answer the following questions:

- What do you really want from your life?
- What are you willing to stop and start to get what you want for your life?
- Who's counting on you?

"If destruction fails to entangle us, distraction will do its best."

—Beth Moore, author and Bible teacher

Many times, the things we think we are sacrificing are really just distractions to keep us from our truest path. Look back over your list. Can you see how several of the things you wrote down have just been distractions? Some of them are probably adding no value to you whatsoever. Our world is congested with distractions, and you might be surprised to learn that our brains are programmed to respond to them. By default, we are easily distracted by anything that will bring pleasure, anything that may feel threatening, or even something new. When we focus on something new, we have what is called "novelty bias." This is one of many instances where our brain floods with dopamine.

The following information comes from an article by Trevor Haynes, a research technician in the Department of Neurobiology at Harvard Medical School. *"The human brain contains four major dopamine 'pathways,' or connections between different parts of the brain that act as highways for chemical messages called neurotransmitters. Each pathway has its own associated cognitive and motor (movement) processes. Three of these pathways—the mesocortical, mesolimbic, and nigrostriatal pathways—are considered our 'reward pathways' and have been shown to be dysfunctional in most cases of addiction. They are responsible for the release of dopamine in various parts of the brain, which shapes the activity of those areas. The fourth, the tuberoinfundibular pathway, regulates the release of a hormone called prolactin that is required for milk production."*[4]

Smartphones and social media are the superhighways for short-term dopamine loops. The smartphone itself is not addictive, but rather our attachment to the likes and the societal stimulation we receive by seeing who looked at us today. Who watched our story. Who visited our page and left a comment on a post we wrote. We, at our core, have a desire to be loved. This is what we are seeking the most. We also have a need to identify. Social media is used for both.

However, studies are showing that smartphones, and specifically social media, are now tied to an increase in anxiety, depression, sleep issues, and car accidents. Not only are we distracted by social media, but the phone calls and the text messages that come in have us very distracted. We take our phones into meetings and keep them on the table at dinnertime, which is distracting. Students bring them to class and use them while in the class. They think we can't see them, but we can, and this professor right here will call you out if you spend too much time on it, that is for sure. I don't mind them, but I don't let them stay out for long. They are in our cars, and we swear we can drive and text. But the truth is we cannot do that and actually be safe. Why is it that we don't think we can wait to stop to respond? Do you know?

Here are some reasons: We think we can multitask. Nope! That is an illusion. The brain can only focus on one thing at a time. When you are multitasking, your brain is actually switching back and forth, delaying what you are doing and your response time to it. We think we have to be plugged in all the time. This, too, is a lie. You don't need to always be on, always available. No! Here is the biggest one of all: our self-esteem feeds on social responses, as well as our response to others. We often feel an urgency that is not there to respond to others even though it puts us in jeopardy or takes us away from what we really need to be focusing on.

The reason I went in so much on the smartphone and social media is because I know these are some of our biggest distractions and ones that we need to spend more time sacrificing. Another reason is I want you to learn as much about the brain as you can. To live the Empowered Life, you will be rewiring your brain. You are pulling off old programming and establishing new patterns. I want you to learn how your brain works in conjunction with your world and what you have in your world. Maybe social media is not an issue for you. This may be the case. But maybe you are a people-pleaser and, at every turn, you are bending over backwards for someone. You are getting your dopamine hit a different way, but in the end, you are still getting that hit. As I close out this chapter, I am going to leave you with a few tips on how to be free from distractions.

If you know you spend way too much time on social media, then I need you to block at least one time a week not to be on it all. Pick one day and just step away. You will not miss anything, I promise. I even suggest trying a social media fast. You can do it. Replace the time you would be wasting on social media with writing or goal planning. Better yet, get to work. Start moving through your projects. Go for a walk and spend some time in nature. Another tip is to block out time in your day when you can completely focus on you and your goals. The phone is off. Put that sucker on airplane mode. Focus on you. Take inventory of your life, your goals, and where you are.

One of the main reasons why businesses are successful is because they track and look at data constantly. From that data, they can make changes and see what is working and what is not. When you have your intentional reflection time with no distractions, you, too, can see what is working or what isn't in your life. You, too, can make the changes needed. This is how you live the Empowered Life. Another tip is to start saying no to more people. I don't know if you know you have right to your no, but in a few chapters, I am going to share that very important Palumbo Principle with you, and I am expecting you to rise up in it and own your authority and your right. For now, just know that you do have a right to say no.

The work to live EMPOWERED is not easy, but it is worth it. Sacrifices are not going to give you the same dopamine hit as the superhighways of social media, but they will give you a greater lasting effect in your life—one in which you need no rush for. You will be living a life that only others dream of. Why? Because you did the work to create it. You made the sacrifice to not be distracted by people, places, or things. You answered the call to be a generational curse breaker and generational blessing maker. You have chosen to live the Empowered Life, and by doing so, you took the rights to your life back, and the keys are in your hands. No one else's. The sacrifices you make today will be ones that are felt not only for your life, but for future lifetimes that have yet to come. And success will be commanded to follow you and your seeds forevermore.

S E V E N

PALUMBO PRINCIPLE 4:
THE FOUR AGREEMENTS

"Every human is an artist. The dream of your life is to make beautiful art."

—Don Miguel Ruiz, author

*T*he Four Agreements, by Don Miguel Ruiz, is a book I highly recommend. My uncle Michael gave me the book several years ago and encouraged me to read it. I ate it right up, and today I tell all my students and clients about it. I have even considered adding it as a course requirement for one of the classes I teach, which deals with society and why we do what we do. Before I share with you what the four agreements are, I will share with you the even deeper message of the book: programming.

We have all been programmed since the moment of conception. Our programming makes us think a particular way. My mentor and dearest friend, Ron Hickey, says it best: *"If you don't have the courage to think critically for yourself, then someone will do the thinking for you, offering nothing substantive for your life. People have a way of pressuring you into complacency and maybe even pushing you into downright wretchedness. Before long, you rationalize your situation and learn to depend on others to do your every thinking."* Well, our parents really did all the thinking for us as children. They wired our brains, as well as the brains of others with whom we had contact. My grandfather, who abused me, certainly wired a lot of my brain. Today, I am successfully rewiring it.

You, too, have been wired, and your programming affects your everyday life. Then you connect with others who have been programmed, and you dance the night away, and even the day if you are so lucky, but many times you just end up dancing with demons. You eventually wake up and realize you have agreed to things you wouldn't truly agree to. The evolution of self and becoming more self-aware is critical in business and in life. Once you begin to understand that you have been bound to agreements that are not yours, you then need to remove them and create new agreements. I call many of the agreements I had "generational curses," which I have broken. The new agreements I make are "generational blessings."

The tools I have provided in this book can be used to help the rewiring of the trauma-infected mind, but it is up to you to do the work. Faith is dead without action. For me personally, *The Four Agreements* helped me begin to rewire my mind. I have now read the book several times. Currently, as I am writing this book, I just launched a book club with a group of women that I am life coaching. They come from tragic backgrounds like me. We are now reading *The Four Agreements* together. This is how we change the narrative. The knowledge we receive is not for us but rather for the one who is in the valley waiting for us to arrive. We don't need to do anything other than share our story, share our truth. In that, we give way for others to come as they are—to come when they are ready.

One of the things I always say in my speeches is I plant good seed, and if you are ready, you will awaken. And even if you are not, I trust in my seed and know at the right time it will bear great fruit. I am not worried about seeing the fruit; the harvest is undeniable—but only if I surrender to my calling that I am to deliver the message and that is all. Far too often, we want to not only deliver the message but make it happen, too. But it is not our place. Once the message is delivered, you must surrender. You must trust. You must move forward, continuing to deliver more messages. It took me some time to fully understand that. But once I did, well, then came this extraordinary ability to not only speak but write. I encourage you to give way to the gift. Each of us has God-given talents and gifts to share with this world. Don't hide them. We need them now more than ever before.

Let me share with you the four agreements as they are written by the author himself, after which I am going to break them down, Professor Palumbo style.

The Four Agreements are:

1. *"**Be Impeccable with Your Word.** Speak with integrity. Say only what you mean. Avoid using words to speak against yourself or to gossip about others. Use the power of your Word in the direction of truth and love.*

2. ***Don't Take Anything Personally.** Nothing others do is because of you. What others say and do is a projection of their own reality, their own dream. When you are immune to the opinions and actions of others, you won't be the victim of needless suffering.*

3. ***Don't Make Assumptions.** Find the courage to ask questions and to express what you really want. Communicate with others as clearly as you can to avoid misunderstandings, sadness and drama. With just this one agreement, you can completely transform your life.*

4. ***Always Do Your Best.*** *Your best is going to change from moment to moment; it will be different when you are healthy as opposed to sick. Under any circumstance, simply do your best, and you will avoid self-judgment, self-abuse, and regret."*[5]

Oh, the love I have for the first agreement. I don't know about you, but I cannot stand it when someone tells me something and doesn't come through. I struggle with trust anyways due to the depth of trauma I have endured, but I do try to give people the benefit of the doubt. Still, I can be outright pissed off when someone is not intentional with their word. Like, really? How hard is it to keep your word? It cannot be that hard. Shoot, I do it. Oh, but right there is the problem. I am expecting others to be like me. I am expecting them to have the same respect as me. However, this is going to get me nowhere fast. The more I learn about psychology, especially as it relates to trauma, the more of an understanding I have of why people do what they do. Having a deeper understanding allows me to hold greater compassion. So, I get it. Now, it doesn't excuse it, but I do get it. Then I feel even more commission to write and speak and get tools in hurting people's hands so they can heal and be free.

Where being impeccable with your word really comes into play is with self. The way we talk to our self is extremely critical. If you are going to live the Empowered Life, you must be impeccable with your word. There is a voice, and it is not nice at all. It is downright cruel. You know, the one that might've just told you off last night. The one that, in the midst of despair, wants to tear you down even more. That voice must be silenced. That voice must be removed from your inner world. It takes work. As EMPOWERED as I am today, I still hear and deal with that voice. I am, however, much further along in my journey, and I can and do silence it. I work diligently to rewire that part of my brain, and I will never stop till the work is finished.

I encourage you to work on your inner voice. I also encourage you to keep your word with others, and, most importantly, with self. I encourage you to break the curse of "stinking thinking." If you set a goal, then keep it. If you don't keep it, then speak truth over why you didn't keep it. If you tell someone you are going to show up for them, then do it. If you cannot show up, then just tell them. Let them know. Speak with love and truth. Speak with integrity. Lift the vibration of your words, because they are energy, and the universe is listening.

"People will love you. People will hate you. And none of it will have anything to do with you."

—Abraham Hicks, author

The second agreement is, for me, by far the hardest. I have to remind myself often not to take anything personally—not the good nor the bad. This can be difficult. As humans, we seek validation. We, at our core, have a desire to be loved and accepted. But we can become entangled in others' opinions of us, and down the rabbit hole we go. All too often, we base our self-worth on whether someone thinks we are pretty enough or smart enough. Just because someone perceives you a certain way doesn't mean you should own that perception. What others say is often a reflection of them, not you.

So, how do you keep the agreement to not take anything personally? You recognize that, since birth, we have been brainwashed and programmed into thinking that we must belong. We must fit in. So, we worry about what others think about us. You must stop worrying about what others think. We all turn to dust. No one, and I mean no one, is getting out alive. So stop worrying. I need you to own who you are and really own it. Be confident. You are a child of God. You need no further approval. I need you to be so focused on building your empire and your generational wealth that you have no time to care what others think. I need you to stop giving your power away, either by being inflated by someone's glamourized words or by being downgraded by someone's negative words. Either way, you are giving power away. That can be poison to the soul. Because words are my love language, I can really struggle with this one. But as I have grown in my wisdom, I can tell you this much: the more I stop worrying about others and what they say about me, the better off I am and continue to be. I am, however, a work in progress, and this one will be the one I will need to work on the most. This is a marathon, not a sprint.

The third agreement is one that is super important—more so for women than men. Women are some of the best investigators out there. We just know what we know, and you cannot tell us differently. However, unless we have asked questions, we are just making assumptions, and that can get us in trouble. We are not mind readers. We don't know it all. And yes, though we might have a gut feeling about something, we still need to do our due diligence and fact check. Ask questions, and fully investigate. Remember, truth doesn't require you to believe it to be truth, only a lie represented as truth does so. When seeking truth, in time, it does appear. Just be bold enough to ask the hard questions. Many times, we are not bold enough to ask those hard questions, so we ask them and answer them in our minds. Then, we sit there and suffer in torture with answers we created that may be wrong. Give someone the benefit of the doubt. Allow others the space to tell their side of the story. As a professor, I am always pushing my students to think for themselves. In order to do that, one must ask questions. What I have found is people generally struggle to ask questions. Therefore, they tend to make assumptions.

There are no dumb questions, and if you truly want to know something, you must ask. You must seek the answer. This one agreement will save you many a headache, and, as the author states, "*With just this one agreement, you can completely transform your life.*"

I love the fourth agreement the most because it is hard to live the other three agreements. However, I can tell you from personal experience—and with full confidence—that when you do live the other three, they hold great freedom. You become a spiritual warrior, and you ultimately become a master of self. Ruiz has written several other books called the Mastery series, and I have read a few of them as well. Because one of my main issues has been self-hatred, I was drawn to one book in his series called *The Mastery of Love*, which is a collection of stories all geared toward exposing and enlightening one on self-love. In the next chapter, I am going to share a story from *The Mastery of Love* with you.

My dear one, the way out is within, and we are to love ourselves. This can be a struggle for so many. So, we say things we don't mean and make promises that get broken. We are not impeccable with our word. We take things personally because we seek approval from others, not realizing that we all turn to dust and the only approval needed was given to us the moment God had created us. We make assumptions and then in rolls drama, lack of understanding, and poor communication. All we need is knowledge. Without it, we perish. So remember to love yourself daily. Do your best to live in new agreements you have set, and never be afraid to seek knowledge and understanding. Hold compassion for yourself daily because we don't always get it right. To live this life is hard. But to live EMPOWERED is very possible.

E I G H T

"May all your days be filled with twinkles so bright that even in the darkest depths you shine brightly."

—Carmela Dutra, author

The very last story I share with my students is the story of the star. I also usually share it as my closer for workshops and speaking engagements. For me, the story of the star truly resonated. As I stated in the previous chapter, it comes from *The Mastery of Love* by Don Miguel Ruiz.[6] It is one of my most favorite stories in the book.

The story is about a man who was very intelligent. He would travel around the world and speak to all kinds of people from many nations. His message: *Love does not exist.* He would teach people the notion that love, as we know it, is not love. One day, the man was walking in a park, and along the trail he was walking upon, he came across a woman weeping on a park bench. He was taken by her and was concerned as to why she was weeping. He sat next to her ever so gently and inquired why she was weeping so.

The first thing she said was, "Love does not exist." He was taken aback because he spent the majority of his time convincing people that love does not exist, and here this woman was telling him what he told others. He inquired again, "How do you know that love does not exist?" She replied, "It could not. I loved my husband, or so I thought I did, and I thought he loved me too. I did everything he asked of me. I dressed the way he wanted. I cooked the way he liked. We had two beautiful children and I raised them the way he told me to. I did everything the way he instructed, and he left me after our youngest son left for college. Love does not exist. It is an illusion." The man replied, "You are correct, my dear. Love does not exist."

Now the man and the woman had this agreement that love did not exist, and they became friends. They would meet at the park regularly and share the day with each other. It didn't matter if they were having a good day or a bad day. They each accepted each other as they appeared from day to day. At that point, they were both operating in their authentic selves. There was no pressure to be anything other than the lily in the valley, as God designed them to be.

The days increased from meeting a few times a week to meeting almost daily. They truly enjoyed each other's company and began to wonder what they were really experiencing. Could it have been love they were experiencing, they questioned? So, they decided to become even closer because, of course, that is when it all changes, you know. They became a couple, and guess what? Nothing changed. They were their authentic selves. There was no pressure to be anything other than who they were.

So, they decided to take it even one step further. Because at this point, perhaps, love really did exist. But of course, marriage would surely kill it. So, they gave marriage a try. Yet again, they fell even more deeply in love. They had actually found love. They had found love in themselves to be who they were—their authentic selves. There was no pressure to be anything other than the lily in the valley, as God created them to be.

The man and the woman lived a very long life. When they were in their 90s, the man and woman were outside, and they were looking at the heavens. All of a sudden, a star appeared in the sky, and it headed right to the man. The most beautiful star you have ever seen was floating down ever so softly, and it landed in the man's hands. He was so taken by the star, but he loved the woman so much he wanted to give her the star. He turned toward her, and with the biggest smile on his face, he reached out his hand and placed the star in hers. The moment it landed in her hands she immediately dropped it, and the star shattered into a thousand pieces.

Why did it shatter, you ask? Because the star was never intended for her. The star was intended for him. She would have received her own star.

I need you to understand that you are a star holder. But the moment you place your star in anyone else's hands, it will shatter. What is so awesome about our God is that He takes our broken star, puts it back together again, and we have a stained-glass star that can still shine. But it must be in our own hands to shine. I know you want others to see how amazing your star is, and you just want them to touch it, but they cannot. If they do, they release the grip of their own star and will not shine. Far too often, I placed my star in others' hands, and it shattered. Then I took my power back; I became emotionally intelligent, and I learned the power of delayed gratification. I made sacrifices, which included letting go of people and things that caused me more harm than good. I pulled away from agreements I never agreed to in the first damn place, and I began operating the best I could in the four agreements. I picked up my star, and I began to shine. I became EMPOWERED!

I need you to understand that when you are holding your star and shining, two things are going to happen. You will intimidate others. You just will. I have found this to be true more so with women than men. Women sometimes struggle to trust or like other women. This comes from a deep wound that can often stem from motherhood. We not only have daddy issues in our world, but we also have a very big mommy issue. The sisterhood is deeply broken and wounded. But she is healing, and she will return to her rightful place in the world. But we must move past being intimidated when others shine. We must understand that just because someone else is winning or shining doesn't mean we are not.

I am a very bright light; I have even been called a beacon—one who leads people to the light. But I can also tell you that many times my feelings have been deeply hurt by others because they didn't like how brightly I shined. As if I was taking their light. But I was just holding my star. As I put the four agreements into practice, specifically not to take anything personally, I became more confident in myself and my star. I grew in self-love, and I was able to learn the truth. Those who are intimidated by me, well, it is not really them but the darkness that is within them—the trauma they have. Light is not intimidated by light; only darkness is. This is why it is so important to apply the principles and live the Empowered Life. It allows you to heal, and those who heal don't hurt others. Please understand that hurt people hurt people. You know you have truly healed when someone strikes you with hurtful words, deeds, or actions, and you no longer respond. You hold peace. This takes work and a lot of it. But the more you heal by doing the hard work, the more freedom you receive. But remember, freedom comes in pieces.

Now on the other side of the coin, when you are holding your star, you will attract other star holders. And what a beautiful community it will be. It will be love. When I really buckled down and stopped putting my star in other people's hands and let go of toxic people, places, and things, I spent some time in what one may call a void, but it was just a hallway. As the saying goes, when one door closes, another one opens. I can clearly remember God telling me that I had to let go of so many. He reminded me that the Queen of England doesn't just go anywhere. Oprah doesn't just have any friends. Oh no. They are set apart and for a reason. They keep a particular energy around them. They must. That is the calling on their lives, and if they don't honor that, well, they would not only lose their power and purpose, but so many other people they are accountable for would not receive what they need. The same is true for each of us, as we each are accountable for others. This ranges per person and life story. For me, I am meant to serve millions. I have seen them coming in visions. I suffered for a really long time in order to be used in such a way. My suffering and your suffering is not in vain. You are His glory. You can rise up, and you must.

You must hold your star and the other star holders will appear. For me, I call them "GWOMEN." GWOMEN is a group of special women who can be found across this nation and even overseas. When I began my speaker training, I joined a group called Grindation, led by Kendall Ficklin. And his beautiful, ever-so-talented wife, Karen Ficklin, leads GWOMEN. Now, at first, I didn't want anything to do with the women. I was scared. My history with women has been rocky. They can be intimidated by me, and then my feelings get hurt because I have a very big heart and I truly love others. I have had female friends, but for the most part, they have been unhealthy—my best friend being the exception.

I did make a connection with one of the other lead women in GWOMEN, and my first conversation with her was, "Do I really have to hang with the ladies?" She laughed and said she would be a very rich woman if she had a dollar for every time she heard that. She encouraged me to give it a chance. I thought to myself, *Okay, maybe this time will be different. Let's just see.* So I jumped in, and, to my surprise, there before me were some of the most amazing women I had ever encountered. I had found star holders because I, too, was holding my star. And after spending some time in the hallway (aka the void), the door opened. My tribe had arrived. I could truly trust these women, and that was big for me. This led to greater healing. Because of the GWOMEN and the healing I have received by being in this beautiful community, I, by His perfect design, am moving forward on a mission to heal the feminine spirit. I am taking a tour this year, and this book you are reading is going to be included in my workshops. Each woman who attends will receive this book along with several other things that I pray will bless them on their journey to live the Empowered Life.

My tour will be geared toward women and young girls. My daughter will be with me, along with my co-host, and she is going to help me EMPOWER women and young girls across this nation. This is how we change the narrative. This is how we break the curse and plant the blessing. We hold our star. We remember we are love, and we understand that in that lies great purpose— everlasting purpose. Love is the only thing that is real. Everything else is an illusion. Love never dies, but it does transcend, as each of us will do one day. So, LOVE, because that is what you are! And remember, you are a star holder. I leave you now with a poem I am sure you know all too well. But I bet you only know part of it. I used to sing it to my daughter when she was in my womb. I want you to read all the words and let it set in your spirit a little. Then, in the space provided, I would like for you to journal about the beautiful star that you are.

"Twinkle, twinkle, little star,
How I wonder what you are!
Up above the world so high,
Like a diamond in the sky.

When this blazing sun is gone,
When he nothing shines upon,
Then you show your little light,
Twinkle, twinkle, through the night.

Then the traveler in the dark
Thanks you for your tiny spark;
He could not see where to go,
If you did not twinkle so.

In the dark blue sky you keep,
And often through my curtains peep,
For you never shut your eye
Till the sun is in the sky.

As your bright and tiny spark
Lights the traveler in the dark,
Though I know not what you are,
Twinkle, twinkle, little star."

—"Twinkle, Twinkle, Little Star" by Jane Taylor

I want you to read the poem over one more time. Let the words fully digest. There is so much meaning in this one poem. You see, if we don't twinkle, the traveler in the dark cannot see the way. Many times, we are the traveler in the dark. And by others holding their star, it allows us to see our way. So hold your star and give light to those who cannot yet see. Now take some time to reflect upon your star. Did you place it in someone else's hand only to watch it shatter? Are you holding it and shining brightly? Just write what comes.

NINE

PALUMBO PRINCIPLE 2:
YOU HAVE RIGHTS TO YOUR "NO,"
AND YOUR "YES" IS UNDENIABLE

"Let today mark a new beginning for you. Give yourself permission to say NO without feeling guilty, mean, or selfish. Anybody who gets upset and/or expects you to say YES all of the time clearly doesn't have your best interest at heart. Always remember: You have a right to say NO without having to explain yourself. Be at peace with your decisions."

—Stephanie Lahart, author

D id you know that you have rights to your "no"? So many people don't know this simple truth. For me, my "no" was taken at the age of three. Because my "no" was stolen, I didn't know how to say, *"No, don't touch me." "No, don't beat me." "No, don't treat me like that." "No, you can't have my money." "No, I can't take you there or here or everywhere."* And if you told me no, I would be crushed. *"No, I don't love you." "No, I can't help you." "No, you didn't get that job."* And so on.

As an entrepreneur, we often get told no. And in order to make it in this game, you must be able to handle it. I, for the most part, did. But when it came to matters of the heart, I really struggled. I have many a story I could share, but the one I'll share with you now is my journey to becoming a professor. After a long, hard-fought battle to keep my business afloat, I knew I needed to do something else. I had a meeting with Dan, the man I had worked for and bought my business from. He encouraged me to look into an MBA or a JD (Juris Doctorate). Sac State just happened to have an informational session on an MBA/JD split degree. I thought, *How fitting. Let me go check this out.* The event ended up hosting several programs. EMBA was one. As I finished up with the MBA/JD, I scurried over to the EMBA. EMBA stands for **E**xecutive **M**aster's in **B**usiness **A**dministration. After learning about the program, I knew right then that it was for me. I'd already had prior knowledge that if I earned my MBA, I would qualify to teach at the college level.

If you recall me telling you earlier, I initially was going to school to be a high school photography teacher, so I had a K-12 background that served me well. I had been teaching for free for about a decade. I thought, *Wow, this is it. I am going to be a college professor. That is my next level, and all I have encountered thus far will be shared with so many. I will be able to give back.* So, I applied to the EMBA program and was accepted. That was an undeniable YES! And it was mine. Oh, I was so elated. I graduated in 2010 and hit the ground running. I knocked on door after door. I had meetings with deans, department chairs, and other professors, all in pursuit of securing a teaching position. But time and time again, I was told no.

Then I found out that Los Rios Community College District had a faculty internship program. This program was designed to give up-and-coming professors a chance to get it. I found out about it three days after it had closed. But I am gritty, so it didn't deter me one bit. Oh no, I waited, and when it opened again, I jumped right on it. I submitted my paperwork and application. I received a call that I was going to be interviewed. *Oh boy,* I thought, *this is it! I am in now.* But guess what came rolling in...a NO! I had the interview, but to be honest with you, I didn't do very well. I forgot to say my name when doing the teaching demo, and I was not as polished as I normally am. It stung to receive the rejection email, but again, I am gritty, and I am a LION. I waited, and year three came around, the internship opened again, and I was all ready to go. I might've been the first person to apply. When it opened, I jumped. Again, I received a call that I was going to receive an interview. I thought to myself, *This time is your time, Natasha. You got this.* I

119

went into the interview confident, polished, and I blew the teaching demo out of the water. And for my closer, I explained to my interviewer, Dolly, that I had been waiting for this internship for three years. She replied, "Three years? Wow." I said, "Yes, and I sure hope my wait is now over."

Well, it wasn't too much longer after that when I received the email letting me know that I had been accepted. My undeniable YES had arrived yet again. At this point, it was 2015. I graduated in 2010. It took me five years to get to my internship. That is a long time to wait. This is why when I tell you to stay gritty, baby, I mean it. It took grit to stay in the game. And it still does take grit to do all that I do today. It takes grit to know you can take your NO's and not be moved by them. It takes grit to hold on to the truth that you have an undeniable YES! These are the keys to living the Empowered Life. I really did enjoy my internship, and it validated that, indeed, I was going to be a professor. That was a calling on my life. I had an interview set up during the summer, which I was confident would lead me to a position. My internship was at Sacramento City College. This is the same college I had attended—where my metamorphosis began. It meant everything to be back there and give back. I was truly thriving, and I was so hopeful for the future.

Well, the summer came and was closing out. I had not received a call for the interview. I then inquired, and I was told they had no positions to offer. NO was given to me yet again. But this no felt very different than before. This one took my heart and threw it on the ground and stomped all over it. This one truly hurt. I was devastated, to say the least. I did, however, pick myself up and continued moving forward. I knocked on door after door. I met with more deans, more department chairs, and more professors. Then, my very good friend and mentor, Randy Pench, connected me with a department chair at Sierra College in the photography department. I have two photography degrees. Those, combined with my MBA, also qualify me to teach photography at some schools. I met with the department chair and we had a wonderful meeting. He asked me what I truly wanted to teach. I replied, "Business. I have much experience in business. Yes, I am wonderful at photography and have much knowledge, but I pursued an MBA to teach business."

He then proceeded to walk me over to the business department and introduced me to the dean, who took the time to hear my story. She was so moved, she set me up with an interview shortly after. What I had that she was looking for was experience. What I had gone through, and how I'd grown my business, was exactly what Sierra College was all about teaching. It was a bonus that I had been in the internship, but the sealing of the deal was my experience.

Don't negate your experience. I was hired at Sierra College to teach one class, and before the semester started, they offered me two more, one of which was an entrepreneurship class. My undeniable YES was rolling in, and it was far more powerful and purposeful than any of the NO's I had been told before. Not too long after that, Woodland Community College picked me up. Then a very big moment happened: Sacramento State came in with an offer to teach. For me, giving back is everything. I am a Sac State alumnus, and there I was, back teaching. Full circle yet again.

Shortly after, I received an email from the dean at Cosumnes River College, which is part of the Los Rios District. They had an emergency need for an instructor and guess who was able to fill it? I cried when I received my parking pass and ID card for Cosumnes. These amazing undeniable YES's are what it is all about. When I lost my interview for the internship, I couldn't figure it out. My mentor—the one who told me just stay gritty, baby—well, he also was the one who advised me to go back to SCC and talk to the department chair and find out what happened. He said, "Just tell her to give it to you raw and in the most New York way possible,"—she was a New Yorker—"and let her know, no matter what, you can handle it."

And that is what I did. I can remember it like yesterday. I boldly asked, "What happened?" What she told me had me in total shock. She said, "Natasha, you are too relatable." Then she proceeds to tell me that I didn't have enough empathy. My head was spinning. I said, "What? Not enough empathy? How?" She explained that my mentor had said that I didn't show her empathy when she had to end the semester early due to surgery. Because I was sad that the semester was ending early for me, she took it as me not having empathy for her. This was so far from the truth.

Yes, I did get sad, but I also bought this same woman a gift and card before I left her. I also texted and checked on this same woman before her surgery and after. I also made sure this woman knew how much I appreciated her for allowing me to share space in her classroom. I thought, *Are you kidding me right now?* And then to say I was too relatable, again, are you kidding me? If I cannot get on the ground with you, I cannot reach you. If I cannot reach you, I cannot teach you. I am an educator, and just because I am relatable doesn't mean I don't have boundaries. It doesn't mean that I am not still in charge and the leader of the ship. No, this is exactly why I am a leader. I will not tell you the way; I am going to show you the way.

What really happened is I was holding my star, and this woman was intimated by me. What helped me see this was I had another mentor on campus who was able to sit in on one of the days when I instructed. This mentor teaches teachers. He is an expert in pedagogies, and he told me that what I had was a true gift to teach. I was able to make the autistic student pay attention. I was reaching those whom others could not. Then I learned that not only did I have reviews for the class, but she also went through a review process. Well, my student reviews ended up being better than hers. She didn't take too kindly to this. Again, I was just holding my star, walking in my purpose. I was intimidating, but it was not intentional.

After the internship ended, she proceeded to tell the dean and chair that I had not shown her empathy and that she was concerned I was too relatable to the students. This caused me to lose my interview. But remember, you have rights to your NO, and your YES is undeniable. As badly as this hurt, the truth is that I had rights to the NO. If I had been hired at SCC, I would have been hired for a general business course—not entrepreneurship, which is where my expertise lies. This is why I had to receive that NO. This is why Sierra was my undeniable YES.

Today, not only do I teach entrepreneurship, but I also teach social entrepreneurship. My books, which are titled *Entrepreneurship Empowered, Entrepreneurship Empowered: The Companion Workbook*, and *IMPACT,* are all used in my courses. My students are required to buy them. They are now in the hands of hundreds of students who get to not only read my story, but also grow in the knowledge of entrepreneurship and social entrepreneurship. Those are some pretty beautiful undeniable YES's, wouldn't you say? Here is the real kicker: my first year teaching at Sierra College, I received an award. The reason I won is because I was so relatable to students. Their lives were transforming, and they were satisfied with their care. The school was proud of me for operating out of my gift and empowering the students to do the same.

"And we know that God causes everything to work together for the good for those who love God and are called according to His purpose."

—Romans 8:28

When you become EMPOWERED and take the rights to your life back, this includes taking your rights to saying "no" back. When I took the right back to say no, I realized I had let people walk all over me because I needed to feel like I belonged, that I was loved. But that was not love at all, and it only made me sicker. My trauma side effects almost killed me. But God saw me through, and He will see you through. I stopped being a people-pleaser. I started saying no to others and yes to me. I became EMPOWERED and took my rights back. Being told no means nothing to me anymore because my YES is undeniable.

My ability to say no has made me grow so much. I am much more balanced and healthier now. Here's what is interesting: because I have started saying "no," I am able to serve at a much higher level than before. I have much more to offer in the right way, and with complete purity of heart. I encourage you to remember that you have rights to your "no," and your "yes" is undeniable. There is a time and a season for everything under the sun and in heaven. Your undeniable "yes" is found many times throughout your life and will certainly be found in heaven. You just need to allow that to remain at the forefront of your mind at all times. Your "yes" is far more powerful and purposeful than any "no" you will ever receive. As I stated before, I would be crushed to receive a "no," but my journey to becoming a professor is where I realized that my "yes" is undeniable. This powerful principle changed my life. I use this principle when I am creating my vision. I bring my senses in along with it and feel my undeniable "yes." I feel its power and purpose. I can see the "yes" appearing here and there. I know nothing is going to stop my "yes." Only I can stop it, and far too often, people do, because they don't know how to move past the "no" they just received.

The dice of life will toss you a no time and time again. Your job is to pick up those dice, shake them, spit on them if you must, then throw them back to this world with all you have inside you, and say, "MY YES IS UNDENIABLE!" The power belongs to you. You are to live the Empowered Life!

T E N

"I love those who can smile in trouble, who can gather strength from distress, and grow brave by reflection. 'Tis the business of little minds to shrink, but they whose heart is firm, and whose conscience approves their conduct, will pursue their principles unto death."

—Leonardo da Vinci, Renaissance genius

Y ou are more powerful than you could even possibly imagine. *The way out is within.* No one is coming to save you. It is just that real. You can, however, save yourself. You were created in the image of the Most High God. Then He so graciously placed His lips on yours and blew breath into you. You are the image of the almighty God, and you have His breath in your lungs. What more do you really need?

For so many years, I wandered in the wilderness, searching and searching. One day, I came upon a large wooden door, and carved in the door in gigantic lettering was the word VALIDATION. *Oh boy,* I thought, *that is exactly what I need.* So, I knocked on the door, and all of a sudden, a guard appeared.

"What do you want?" the guard asked.

"Oh, I just want to come through this door."

"NO," the guard yelled back. "Go away."

I hung my head and away I walked. But I was determined to go through that door, so I thought to myself, *The guard will take an offering, I am sure. I will go get everything I can find. I will go dig up gold with my bare hands. I will search and collect, and I will search and collect some more, then I will take all that I have, all that I am, and give them to the guard.*

I returned to the door and knocked. The guard appeared.

"What do you want?"

"I have everything I could gather. I have all the gold I could dig up, I have everything I possess, and I will give it all to you if you just let me through the door."

The guard took everything I had, then said, "No, now go away. You cannot come through the door."

I began to reflect. *Why am I the only one at the damn door? Where is everyone else?* The moment I had that epiphany, the guard stood up and pulled off a mask it was wearing to reveal who it really was. The damn guard was me.

We walk in the valley of validation and travel in the forest of falsehood only to finally realize that the door we so desperately want to walk through is one we are guarding ourselves. *The way out is within.* You must pull the mask off, take a cold, hard look at yourself, and decide that you will no longer seek approval from those who will turn to dust just like you. We all die, my friends. Not one of us gets to stay, nor would we really want to, truth be told. But I am a firm believer that we can build something that will outlast time. This is why I work so hard. This is why I am determined to share with the world what I know and hand over the keys I have used to be free.

I need you to no longer underestimate your willpower. I need you to turn your "I wish" into "I will." Stop making wishes and blowing hot air everywhere. Change your wish to "I will" and then execute. Many of you are still waiting for a wish to come true when all you have to do is make it happen. I am a firm believer that anything is possible, and wishes do come true. But you must be action-oriented. The power of will is extremely important to understand and activate at the highest vibrational frequency. How did God create the world? His WILL. Will is all the power that exists. We don't use enough of it. We become lazy and say a wish or two instead of working our God-given power to manifest the miracles in our life. Once you recognize that your willpower is your God-given power, it will increase and show you more than you could ever begin to wish for.

"I now see how owning our story and loving ourselves through that process is the bravest thing we will ever do."

—Brené Brown, author and researcher

I struggled for the longest time to truly love myself. But over time and by doing trauma therapy, I was able to grow in self-love. I really did think it was going to be like a faucet. You turn it on and boom it stays on. I quickly found out that was not the case. Self-love is a daily act. It took work, and it still does. Though I have healed so much, I still have more healing to do. I am, however, very proud of where I am today in my life. I hold space for myself and allow myself to be human. I understand that for the longest time, what I thought was normal was just an unevolved mind that didn't want to face the truth of a tragic story. But then I began to awaken. I began to shed the shadow. And in doing so, the love of self grew, and I no longer was ashamed of my story.

Just as the quote above states, that is bravery.

I encourage you to be brave. Do the work that you need in order to heal. You will find tools, resources, and guides along the way, but it is up to you to use them.

Again, *the way out is within.* Only you can do the work. No one can do it for you. The work is not going to be easy. You may even become physically ill as you throw up your trauma, but you will no longer live in the pain of it, and you will certainly not die with the demons.

Outside of trauma therapy, I highly recommend you do meditation. Meditation is a key to open the door to crawl deeply within. It took me a minute to really understand the power of meditation. My trainer told me one day that I just needed to give it a try, that it would help with calming me down. He shared a meditation app with me called Insight Timer. He explained that I could do a guided meditation and to just start with a three- or five-minute one. I thought, *Well, how bad could this be? Go on, Natasha, give it a try.* I did, and I made it through.

Now mind you, I cannot sit still to save my life. But it was in sitting still that I was able to save my life. I realized that the main reason why I had struggled before with meditation was because of needing to be still. When you are abused or raped, many times, you are forced to be still. The same thing happens with other types of sexual abuse. The same thing happens when you are being beaten. The same thing happens when someone is verbally abusing you or emotionally abusing you. You are stuck in that abuse. For someone who was abused, as a direct side effect, you may just have the can't-sit-still-*ites;* you must always be moving. This is because you are in fight or flight and always prepared for something to happen. I mean, I will still rock my legs just to have movement to this day, and I always want to be on the move. This is deeply intertwined in my makeup, and it is trauma.

But I did it. I committed to doing meditation. It was slow at first, but then I was able to go for longer periods of time, and then I didn't even need the guide anymore. I could sit in stillness, and don't you know that is where the power is! I was finally within, and I was not afraid to be there. I have met my higher self in meditation. I have seen past present and future in meditation. There is so much power to be found when we crawl within. I promise it truly is the way out. It can be scary; I am not even going to act like it is not. But you can and will move past your fear. You must if you are going to live the Empowered Life. I want you to learn all you can about not only meditation but also deep breathing—both of which help calm our nervous system. I want you to take the time to love yourself. This is your life, and you are now taking the keys to your rights back, the keys to your life back.

If you recall from an earlier chapter, we live only in the now. The now is a merry-go-round. Around and around we go. We are timeless yet reside in a time constraint vessel. When we are able to master our now, we truly arrive at a place of enlightenment. When we take time to be still and meditate, we are honoring our timeless being. We are able to remove fears that we are inadequate. We are able to find strength for the moments we are in and the ones to come. We lift ourselves outside of the fragile shell we reside in, and we float around in the abyss of true freedom. You cannot take your mind with you. You must leave that on the playground of life. You cannot take your limitations with you; they will only distract you from the power of what will be revealed to you. You really cannot take anything with, and while lifted and in the core of your heart, you must just allow yourself to see. I promise you what you will see is a sight beyond this world. You will experience a peace unlike anything you have experienced before. The silence will not scare you but rather kiss you ever so softly, and I promise you that it will be unlike any kiss you have ever had before.

This inner calling to your heart is one you should visit often. In our world, we have a heart issue. It is the heart that is deeply broken. People are dying due to heart conditions. This is a curse like any other I have seen because it is the heart that allows us to truly be connected to the source—to God, to the universe, to the multiverse, to it all. That is all we need to be connected to. Everything else will fall into place.

Now I want you to take some deep breaths with me. I don't want you to focus on anything other than your breathing. Breathe in for a seven count, hold for an eight-count breath, then exhale for a seven count. This is a very deep breath, pulling all the way to your core. Do this at least three to four more times. Then, I want you to allow yourself to focus on your heart. Let go of any thoughts. They will come, but don't hold them. Let them float like a cloud. Clouds do not stay; they float away. So do thoughts. We are the ones who keep thoughts captive. We are the ones who hold on to them and rehearse them like lines to a play. But you don't need that script anymore. Surrender the thoughts. Surrender the emotions. Just be still and silent. This may take some time to get used to, and that is okay. I just need you to try. Deep breathing, heart-centered, and in stillness—this is your key. This is the most powerful one of them all because this is where you will find the truest you yet. The one you have always been. The one you will always be. Give it a try and, in the space provided, make some notes of what comes to you. *The way out is within.*

_____

_____

_____

_____

_____

_____

_____

_____

_____

_____

_____

_____

"Your days are numbered. Use them to throw open the windows of your soul to the sun. If you do not, the sun will soon set, and you with it."

—Marcus Aurelius, *The Emperor's Handbook*

I don't know how many days you will have remaining. Not one of us knows that information. But I encourage you not to waste any more days trapped in trauma, shamed by your story. No, my dear one. I am calling you out to the light. I believe you can do it. I believe you can overcome anything this life throws at you. But *the way out is within.* Love is the only thing that is real. Everything, and I mean everything else, is an illusion. Love never dies, but it does transcend, as each of us will do one day. I am now going to close you out with three final call-to-action activities. Make sure to spend some time with each of them.

In the space provided, you are going to write your personal empowerment statement. For your empowerment statement, I want you to tell me what area in your life you would like to be more *EMPOWERED.* What steps will you take to become more *EMPOWERED?* I have shared my personal empowerment statement as an example.

Empowered Statement—My Example:

I am a people-pleaser and many times have become so hurt by family, friends, and people in general. What I am learning is that it is very unhealthy to be a people-pleaser. It can actually make you sick. The side effects of abuse are nothing nice. Being a people-pleaser is one of my side effects. But I am healing and will continue to heal and be free. I have decided to be *EMPOWERED* and no longer subject myself to people-pleasing. I will choose to say "no" and have no remorse. I will say "YES" to me! I am confident in myself and the purpose of my life. I know that I am not able to please everyone, nor will I inspire everyone, but I have had visions where I have seen seas upon seas of people who will be inspired by my life story. I will be used to give hope to so many that feel hopeless. I will be used to help heal and set others free. This pleases me.

Now, it is your turn....

_____

_____

_____

_____

_____

_____

_____

_____

_____

_____

"The time will come
when, with elation
you will greet yourself arriving
at your own door, in your own mirror
and each will smile at the other's welcome,

and say, sit here. Eat.
You will love again the stranger who was yourself.
Give wine. Give bread. Give back your heart
to itself, to the stranger who has loved you

all your life, whom you ignored
for another, who knows you by heart.
Take down the love letters from the bookshelf,

the photographs, the desperate notes,
peel your own image from the mirror.
Sit. Feast on your life."

—"Love After Love" by Derek Walcott

That is a powerful poem, is it not? The part that moved me the most was *"give back your heart to itself, to the stranger who has loved you all your life, whom you ignored for another..."* I don't know about you, but I can attest to ignoring me for another. But when I gave my heart back to myself, well, then I could look in the mirror and there I saw beauty. There I saw the one who had

been with me all my days and the one who will continue
to be with me. There I saw the love of God. Now I am
learning to feast on my life—the Empowered Life. The
next call-to-action activity is a love letter to yourself. I
want you to understand that forgiveness is the key to
your awakening. You are learning how to heal your
emotional energy, your trauma, and the ancestral train of
trauma that has been passed down to you. In the space
provided, write. Freely allow the words of love to flow
from the heart. Then make sure to go back and read it
over.

It took me many years to finally pull the muzzle off my mouth and live out loud. I have an extraordinary God-given talent, which is to give others the gift of self. I give you the tools to help you find your authentic self. In doing so, I have given you everything you need. Like a domino effect, after you truly grasp hold of the gift of you, everything else will fall into place. I firmly believe the call-to-action activities you have encountered thus far have revealed a deeper you. Before I close us out in our final call-to-action activity, I want to take the time to thank you for reading this book, and even more so for trusting me to act as a guide for you as you do the work to heal yourself and walk in your freedom. One of the things I do with my writings is I project myself forward to hold space for my readers. I know that many of the things I have asked you to do are challenging. You may have even skipped over a few, some, or all, but I encourage you to do the work now. I have space held for you, and you are supported. It is up to you to do it. *The way out is within.*

I am truly honored to do the work I have been called to do. I suffered a very long time, and I promise I would suffer all over again just for you. Today I live the Empowered Life. Suffering is necessary until it is no longer necessary. Don't ever negate your suffering. Because I suffered, I now get to see lives being transformed. I see healing being released. I see trauma turning into triumph. I see generational curses being broken, and generational blessings being planted. I see that the last legacy is more than just a dream. That, indeed, is what we leave behind as remnants. From dust we came, and to dust we will return. But oh, my dear, God takes ashes and makes beauty. We are timeless, and we are beautiful. Now take some more deep breaths and get ready for your final call-to-action activity. I am now going to task you with the writing of a legacy letter.

Writing a legacy letter is one of the hardest things I have ever done. While earning my master's degree, a professor gave us the assignment to write a legacy letter. I had never heard of such a thing. I can clearly see myself weeping like a baby at my desk as I wrote my son a final goodbye. You see, that is what a legacy letter is. It is a letter from you to your legacy—to your family and friends. You project yourself to your death bed, then you write. It can be very hard, emotionally, because no matter how strong your faith is, the sting of death is very real. We all will cross it one day. I am a true believer that love is the only thing that is real; everything else is an illusion. Love never dies, but it does transcend, as each of us will do one day. I believe we have been given one commission here on earth, and that is to love, and we screw it up every day and three times on Sunday. This is why I share my message. This is why I live out loud. This is why the EMPOWERED series is within me. It is in my writings that I get to live—and the same is true for you. So, I encourage you to write. I desire to see you live the Empowered Life. It is why I give you key after key to help set you free. Though this call-to-action activity is hard and may be difficult to do, I encourage you to write the letter. Go to your death bed, what type of life did you live? What do you want to say to your children and loved ones? What do you wish to say to the future generations still yet to come? What stories, values, wisdom, and blessings do you wish to share? Just write what comes to you. I pray that you write the letter and receive yet another key. Remember, *the way out is within.* Go within and write the letter, then go forward and live the Empowered Life.

_____

_____

_____

_____

_____

_____

_____

_____

_____

_____

_____

_____

_____

_____

_____

_____

_____

_____

About the Author

Ms. Palumbo is a business professional with more than 20 years of experience, 17 as an entrepreneur. She is a creative leader with in-depth knowledge and expertise applying strategic business management, development of small business initiatives, and progressive leadership. Ms. Palumbo is an effective communicator with an innate ability to engage and hold the attention of those she trains and teaches. She owns several businesses, and she successfully grew her core business into multiple states. She is a social entrepreneur and has been serving the homeless community for more than 16 years. In addition to being an Empowered Entrepreneur, Ms. Palumbo is a Business Adjunct professor for several colleges in the greater Sacramento region.

Natasha M Palumbo, MBA
Author, Coach, Consultant and Speaker
Entrepreneur – Educator – Empowered

Instagram and LinkedIn: Natasha M Palumbo
www.natashapalumbo.com

References and Resources

The following resources were used in writing this book and are duly noted in the text:

[1] Waters, Rob. (2019.) "California Surgeon General Puts Spotlight on Childhood Trauma." California Health Care Foundation. Accessed March 12, 2020.
https://www.chcf.org/blog/california-surgeon-general-puts-spotlight-on-childhood-trauma/.

[2] "Art Therapy." (n.d.) Psychology Today. Accessed March 12, 2020.
https://www.psychologytoday.com/us/therapy-types/art-therapy#:~:text=.

[3] "What is Brainspotting and How Does it Work?" (n.d.) Depression Alliance. Accessed March 12, 2020.
https://www.depressionalliance.org/brainspotting/.

[4] Haynes, Trevor. (2018.) "Dopamine, Smartphones & You: A Battle for Your Time." Harvard University: The Graduate School of Arts and Sciences. STIN. Accessed March 12, 2020.
http://sitn.hms.harvard.edu/flash/2018/dopamine-smartphones-battle-time/.

[5] Ruiz, Don Miguel. (1997.) *The Four Agreements: A Practical Guide to Personal Freedom.* Amber-Allen Publishing, Inc. San Rafael, California.

[6] Ruiz, Don Miguel. (1999.) *The Mastery of Love: A Practical Guide to the Art of Relationship: A Toltec Wisdom Book.* Amber-Allen Publishing, Inc. San Rafael, California.

EMPOWERED
LIFE™

Made in the USA
Middletown, DE
15 June 2022

67062399R00099